# THE PSYCHOLOGY OF DOG OWNERSHIP

What are the benefits of owning a dog on health and well-being? Why does a 'problem dog' behave as it does and how can owners deal with unwanted behaviour? How do dogs communicate with humans and each other?

*The Psychology of Dog Ownership* explores the nature of our unique relationship with dogs and its effect on our mental and physical welfare. The book uses psychological learning theory to examine dog behaviour and highlights the importance of determining between typical dog behaviour and behaviour disorders that need treatment.

Focusing on how dog owners can communicate effectively with their pets, and always with the dog's best interests in mind, *The Psychology of Dog Ownership* enhances our understanding of the modern human-canine bond and shows how important and enjoyable this relationship can be.

**Dr Theresa Barlow** has conducted canine research at the University of Southampton and has personally dealt with hundreds of cases of problem pet behaviour having worked in Pet Behaviour for over 22 years. She has specialised in dog aggression and presented her research findings at veterinary and behavioural conferences nationally and internationally.

**Craig Roberts** is a teacher trainer and author of psychology textbooks for A-Level and GCSE. He has been teaching for over 20 years and is an experienced examiner with a number of national and international examination boards.

# THE PSYCHOLOGY OF EVERYTHING

People are fascinated by psychology, and what makes humans tick. Why do we think and behave the way we do? We've all met armchair psychologists claiming to have the answers, and people that ask if psychologists can tell what they're thinking. The Psychology of Everything is a series of books which debunk the popular myths and pseudo-science surrounding some of life's biggest questions.

The series explores the hidden psychological factors that drive us, from our subconscious desires and aversions, to our natural social instincts. Absorbing, informative, and always intriguing, each book is written by an expert in the field, examining how research-based knowledge compares with popular wisdom, and showing how psychology can truly enrich our understanding of modern life.

Applying a psychological lens to an array of topics and contemporary concerns – from sex, to fashion, to conspiracy theories – The Psychology of Everything will make you look at everything in a new way.

Titles in the series:

For further information about this series please visit
www.thepsychologyofeverything.co.uk

# THE PSYCHOLOGY OF DOG OWNERSHIP

THERESA BARLOW AND CRAIG ROBERTS

Routledge
Taylor & Francis Group

LONDON AND NEW YORK

First published 2019
by Routledge
2 Park Square, Milton Park, Abingdon, Oxon OX14 4RN

and by Routledge
52 Vanderbilt Avenue, New York, NY 10017

Routledge is an imprint of the Taylor & Francis Group, an informa business

British Library Cataloguing-in-Publication Data
A catalogue record for this book is available from the British Library

Library of Congress Cataloging-in-Publication Data
A catalog record has been requested for this book

ISBN: 978-0-8153-6243-2 (hbk)
ISBN: 978-0-8153-6244-9 (pbk)
ISBN: 978-1-351-11231-4 (ebk)

Typeset in Joanna
by Apex CoVantage, LLC

Bruiser (1988–2001), a flighty indignant mutt, with a low threshold for aggression, made me question, why do dogs do the things they do? Zara (2006–2017), a tranquil, attentive hound, who was often behaviourally more feline than canine, provided several answers. If in my lifetime, I could have one dog expressing in equal portions "I've got you" like Bruiser did and "I get you" like Zara did, then I would have the perfect dog. Zara and Bruiser, still missed, I imagine you both on a rainbow bridge with those perfect puppies.

Dr Theresa Barlow

During the writing of this book I lost two animals dear to me. One was a three-year-old racehorse called Kenyan who had a zest for life, training and racing. The other was a stray cat, Gigolo, who visited us for years before one night choosing our house as his final refuge from some horrific leg injuries which ultimately was his final night with us.

Craig Roberts

"Man himself cannot express love and humility by external signs, so plainly as does a dog" – Charles Darwin

Source: Erin Broadbent

# CONTENTS

# *PREFACE*

This book examines Anthrozoological research and presents the development of our unique relationship with dogs and the behavioural challenges faced since dogs have been domesticated. The structure and content of this book is aimed at the dog-owning population but the text also aims to serve as useful background reading to those studying introductory level animal-related courses such as animal management and animal care. It will address the links between learning theory and practice enabling the reader to question and appreciate the effectiveness of the techniques used by trainers, behaviour counsellors and indeed the contemporary dog owner. The content touches on the all-encompassing considerations around the impact of evolution and domestication on the development and learning of dogs and how this has formed their responses to human behaviour and endeared them to us today.

The psychology of dog ownership combines the applied psychological theory with the research, practice and teaching of two authors resulting in a book based on a combined 40 years of experience and that aims to offer a taste of why and how dogs and their owners relate. Since the achievement of a BSc in Animal Science, an MSc in Animal Welfare and a PhD in Canine Behaviour and working with hundreds of cases of atypical dog behaviour, my appreciation for a wealth of experience and knowledge is extended. Whilst too many to list here, my gratitude is not only to all the dogs and dog owners I have worked with, but also to all the Animal Ethology lecturers and researchers at Nottingham University, Edinburgh University and Anthrozoology Institute Southampton University (now located to the University of Bristol) for all your help facilitating my research and for your continued endeavours to understand more about the dog-human relationship, I thank you (Dr Theresa Barlow).

A special thank you goes to Erin Broadbent for the dog illustrations used in this book.

The Psychology of Dog Ownership is designed to fit within Routledge's new Psychology of . . . series of concise, engaging and accessible books on areas of popular interest. As part of the series this book focuses on the potential of psychology to enrich our understanding of the human-canine relationship and how companionship has changed to meet the requirements of the contemporary pet owner. Chapter 1 provides an overview of the origins of the modern human-canine bond and how history, science and psychology have resulted in changes in the expectations of our dogs' behaviour today (Dr Theresa Barlow). Chapter 2 is a chronological exploration of our individual relationship with our dog in terms of mental and physical experiences. Beginning with childhood, owning a dog may improve empathy and responsibility; however mistreatment of dogs in this age category may signpost to future mental health issues. Both mental and physical health benefits may be seen throughout adulthood and older age for dog owners by alleviating depression, anxiety and loneliness and even reducing blood pressure and other biological markers of good health. Due to the special dog-human relationship and advancement of understanding of dog behaviour, we will also explore how dogs can be used as a 'service' (e.g. diabetes and cancer detection) whilst maintaining positive dog welfare. This chapter aims to provide a critical analysis of behavioural research for the Psychology and Ethology student (Craig Roberts). Chapter 3 considers the communication between dogs and people as if dog owners can understand some of the subtleties in how their dogs communicate with each other, as well as with themselves as their owner (Dr Theresa Barlow). Chapter 4 follows on from the nature and nurture considerations of Chapter 1 and the communicative factors associated with overbreeding in Chapter 3 and explores how knowledge of animal behaviour, as well as consideration to the intimate inter- and intraspecific communication mechanisms, are grounded in psychological learning theory with examples from domestic dogs. This chapter will end with a summation as to why there is no justification for the mystery often paired with animal whispering and how with an understanding of animal communication and learning theory anyone can be a "whisperer" to their dog (Craig Roberts).

In Chapters 5 and 6 both authors use case studies to relate the links between psychological learning theory and relatable examples in the development and treatment of inappropriate behaviour. Having consolidated the virtues of dogs the latter chapters of the text utilise case studies summate the cause, diagnosis and recommended treatment of some behaviour disorders. Consideration is given to pharmacological intervention, rehoming and euthanasia. In Chapter 7 both authors directly recognise that this book is not extensive or mutually exclusive when examining dog behaviour but it may well be a dog owner's or a behaviour student's first step in gaining some insight as to why a 'problem dog' behaves as it does. So for this reason, as well as for animal welfare considerations, the reader will be signposted to qualified and responsible animal behaviour experts and alerted to the dangers of what not to do.

"Brothers and sisters I bid you beware of giving your heart to a dog to tear"
– Rudyard Kipling

*Source:* Erin Broadbent

# 1

## THE NEW NORMAL OF DOG BEHAVIOUR

The association between humans and dogs is long and varied. Dogs have, and still do, fulfil numerous roles in human society such as security, assistance and companionship. The long-term close association between dogs and humans means that the communication between us as species is well developed. However, frequent misunderstandings still do occur, often resulting in the display of inappropriate aggression and anxiety-related disorders seen in both dogs and their owners. In order to conserve the amicable social bonds between humans and dogs, research into human-animal communication (Anthrozoology), and in particular dog behaviour, is essential for dogs and owners to have a good-natured relationship.

Today just under 44% of UK households own a pet. The most popular is the fish, the second is the dog and the third is the cat. The domestic dog population in the UK is currently estimated at 8.5 million. The size of the dog appears to be an important differentiating factor in the dog owner's choice, with an increase in popularity in the smaller sizes, e.g. French bulldog, Chihuahua and the Pomeranian. There could be a variety of reasons for this. These include the increased cost of living, the challenges many face in stepping on the property ladder, an increase in the number of starter homes and flats with more limited space and/or a delay in starting a family. The rise in demand for small dogs appears to be the compromise dog owners are making given the long-standing knowledge of the benefits of dog ownership. Some of these include the development of empathy and responsibility in children, the cohesion a dog brings to family life and the companionship and social expansion dog ownership brings to the elderly. However, this demand has led to the development of experimental cases and extremism in dog breeding, for example, toy breeds have been bred to fit into cups (tea cup dogs) and there are advertising images of adult toy breeds that are side by side a smartphone demonstrating the "pocket" aspect of the dog. There are the obvious questions around ethics and welfare in promoting a dog as a product rather than a living, breathing being.

However, the rise in popularity of newer dog cross breeds is not always disadvantageous as seen in the fun-loving and even-tempered healthy breeds such as the Cockerpoo (Cocker Spaniel crossed with a Poodle) and the Labradoodle (Labrador Retriever crossed with the Standard, Miniature or Toy Poodle) which are said to have a benefit to owners who are prone to allergies in that these dogs are not likely to cause allergic reactions in humans.

Statistical analysis of the UK Kennel Club breed registrations reflect a significant change in the dog breeding market. During the last four years the population of the toy breeds, for example, the French Bulldogs has exploded, increasing by some 23% whilst the larger breeds, for example, German Shepherd population has reduced by 6% (Figure 1.1). This may not necessarily reflect a reduction in the large dog breeds in the UK as there has also been an anecdotally noted rise in popularity in larger breeds such as the Siberian Husky and the imported wolf dog hybrid. Scientists who study behaviour (Ethologists) have questioned if the changes in the body shape and internal biological mechanisms have been too rapid given archaeological evidence indicates that the dog was only relatively recently domesticated.

The dog was the first species domesticated pre-agriculture and Charles Darwin held the view that all dogs have descended from any one wild species. Archaeological evidence suggests that the dog was domesticated only 12,000 years ago; however there is more recent, genetic

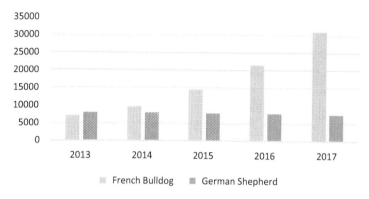

Figure 1.1 Kennel Club breed registrations 2013–2017

evidence suggesting that dogs may have diverged from the wolf (*Canis lupus*) more than 100,000 years ago. The dog's closest relatives could be considered to be the wolf, golden jackal (*Canis aureus*) and coyote (*Canis latrans*) and genetically both the wolf and the dog have very similar anatomy. However, some researchers suggest that the ancestors of both the dog and the wolf became extinct thousands of years ago as there is DNA evidence suggesting that dogs are more closely related to each other than to a wolf, meaning the genetic overlap between dogs and wolves present today is due to interbreeding *after* dog domestication.

There is no absolute consensus as to how dogs were domesticated, but three main ideas exist. The first suggests that the puppies of wild canines were stolen, brought back to the settlement and then bonded to tribeswomen as they suckled at the breasts of lactating mothers. The second theory suggests that dogs were domesticated by scavenging near villages and forming bonds with villagers (there are photographs of village women breastfeeding domesticated animals). These dogs could have been encouraged as their presence would have had several advantages for humans. For example, dogs would have kept the settlement clean by eating human and animal faeces. They also would have barked and growled to warn of the approach of wild animals or human strangers and it is possible that the dogs themselves could have been a valuable source of meat and fur in times of human need (today this is a controversial issue as dog meat festivals are a tradition in parts of the world that many consider inhumane). The third theory of domestication refers to an association with humans at a time when people developed a more settled existence. This would have been at a time when humans were planting crops and storing grain. It would have also been at a time when humans were developing tools into catapults and bow and arrow types, leading to the commencement of hunting and the need for retrieving. Dogs became a very valuable commodity and could be trained and used for tasks, such as the retrieval of prey. However, it is possible that all three methods of domestication may have occurred at similar or different times.

The domestication of the dog has resulted in alterations in how dogs look and behave. The different breeds that exist today are the result of natural genetic mutation and selective breeding. Domestication has led to both the intensification and inhibition of particular behaviour patterns through such selective breeding. An example of the intensification is retrieving and racing, whilst for inhibition there has been a reduction in dog hunting and foraging. In some instances humans have taken the selection of dog breeds to the extreme for entirely aesthetic and/or behavioural purposes.

Selective breeding is considered to have contributed to the health problems associated with specific breeds. If we take the bulldog, for example, its body conformation impacts on its physical and behavioural welfare; mating naturally and successfully is more difficult due to the wide size of the puppies' heads relative to the bitches' pelvis. Excessive wrinkling can home bacteria leading to infection and an overbite can hinder the development of their teeth. Another issue is an obstructive airway due to shortened snout. This affects their ability to maintain their body temperature with exertion. In addition, several eye conditions can occur as a result of their shortened snout and deformity of the spine that at worst leads to loss of function and incontinence could be associated with the curly tail. Behaviourally there have been obstacles as selective breeding for purely aesthetic purposes has resulted in changes in dog body shapes that can impede effective interspecific (between different species) and intraspecific (between the same species) communication.

This can be directly related to misunderstandings – for example, the "perfect double curl" in the tail of a Pug removes the tail as a means of communication which can lead to misunderstandings. Owners can interpret this as inappropriate behaviour or a behaviour problem, the most common of which is aggression. In some cases dogs have been bred specifically to have the body type and/or trained to exhibit the behaviour for heightened aggressive tendencies. When such unethically managed and trained dogs are kept as pets, this poses an obvious risk for the safety of humans and other animals.

## THE HUMAN-CANINE BOND

Historically, dogs may have been chosen as pets because they were able to transfer their social attachments to humans and behave towards people in a manner that we interpreted as approachable, devoted and companionable. Dogs often remain in the vicinity of humans without the need for tethering or other restrictions and display signals indicative of their motivation or state that we interpret correctly. Due to their morphology some dogs are easier to understand than others. For example, a breed such as a Husky is fully equipped with the physical attributes to show their intent. Some of these attributes are pointed ears to move in rotation, fur and colouring to emphasise its status which can be enhanced when hackles are raised and dark liver-coloured lips to contrast teeth to demonstrate levels of arousal. However, a long-haired Pekingese will have to work hard to demonstrate body shapes as these can be disguised by an ample coat and is therefore more likely to use whole body actions and vocalisations to make its intentions known, to compensate for the long hair and small features which can also disguise its signals.

Today the dog continues to be a valuable resource throughout the world as it retains its multiplicity of uses. Examples include:

- Hunting, shepherding, guarding and tracking
- Religious worship, for example, the Aztecs worshipped the dog as having symbolic significance. In addition, in traditional Chinese

astrology, the dog is one of the 12 honoured animals. In Christianity, the Catholic Church recognises Saint Rocco as the patron saint of dogs.

- Scientific research and for ever more sophisticated assistance purposes, medical detection and bomb detection
- Extreme recreational uses, for example, there are extreme dog grooming competitions where groomers dye and sculpt dogs to look like other animals such as a horse, panda or tiger and as a result they are unrecognisable as a breed

However, the dog's primary role today is as our companion and pet and dogs require the cohesion of a predictable social group and when owners are unable to provide such an environment, behaviour disorders can occur. At its most serious, atypical and unacceptable behaviour can be life-threatening for the dog in the sense that if it cannot be tolerated, euthanasia may be considered the owner's only option. The development of behaviour is unfortunately not often the result of one single factor. Behaviour of any dog can be affected by a number of variables during their development. These include:

- The environment, for example, dogs born on a working farm in a rural area find it difficult to adjust when re-homed to an inner-city domestic environment and can experience stress and anxiety
- Physiology, for example, some dogs appear more relaxed than others as a result of the response to their level of stress hormone
- Experience and learning, for example, getting a treat for learning to follow the command of 'sit'
- Genetic predisposition, for example, some dogs are more prone to have particular behaviour patterns such as lethargy or excitability

## DOG BEHAVIOURAL DEVELOPMENT

Development of behaviour is dependent on some significant period of learning. There is typically considered to be a sensitive period of learning between 4 and 16 weeks (socialisation period) in which a puppy learns what to expect from its environment. If, as an adult dog, it comes across novel situations not experienced during socialisation, this can be a cause of stress and could result in what an owner considers inappropriate. The most common disorders seen by Behaviour Consultants are those related to a fear or phobia developed from a bad or inadequate socialisation period (aggressive behaviours are often considered the result of a heighted stress response). A particularly sensitive period is generally accepted as between six and eight weeks of age. During this period the puppy learns to accept the stimuli in its environment as normal. This is therefore considered by breeders as the best time to remove a puppy from its litter enabling the puppy to become familiar with its new environment and the people it will know, as it becomes an adult dog. The socialisation period is important from a behaviour perspective as whatever stimuli the puppy is not exposed to during this period is more likely to trigger a fear response in adulthood. For example, a bad experience such as rough handling by a man can lead to a fear of men in adult life.

## DOG BEHAVIOUR DISORDERS

Some people keep dogs strictly as companion animals rather than for protection or any other functional purposes. As a result there is an increased necessity for the behaviour of the dog to be socially acceptable, for example, today coffee shops are permitting dogs in with their owners. Misunderstandings occur because owners often regard their dog as a more human member of the household and can be upset when the dog behaves in a canine way that does not match the position. Behaviour disorders/problems have been described as being anything that does not fulfil reasonable human expectations including any behaviour that is a source of strain and conflict for the owner, the dog or others. However, these definitions are subjective and do not consider what is typical and atypical behaviour. Potentially any behaviour patterns exhibited by a domestic dog which is considered by the owner as inappropriate or as a problem is a behaviour problem. Such dissatisfaction can jeopardise the completeness of the dog-owner bond. However, it is noteworthy that from the dog's point of view these behaviours could be considered entirely normal, for example, digging holes is an innate dog behaviour and when it is appropriately placed, for example, when digging is in the sand and at the beach, owners rarely have any complaints. However, when their dog digs a hole in their lawn it is problematic to the owner, but it is not an abnormal dog behaviour and therefore this is a problem and not necessarily a disorder. The unwanted behaviour shown by any dog can have multiple causes because of both their innate and learned behaviours. As a result of this the cause, presentation and interpretation of any dog behaviour is ever-changing and depends on the environmental circumstances, the value of any resources that are available and the perceived reward in acquiring the resource. Behaviour disorders include:

- Aggression-related behaviours, can occur interspecifically (between different species) and intraspecifically (within a species)
- Separation-related behaviour such as chewing furniture when left alone at home
- Training issues such as toileting in inappropriate areas of the house
- Phobias such as fear of fireworks
- Stereotypical behaviours such as tail chasing

A most common behaviour disorder is aggression which is multi-faceted. Although behaviour disorders here considered individually, it should be noted that this list is neither mutually exclusive nor exhaustive. For an amenable relationship it is often reported that owning a dog can have advantageous effects on the health and well-being. For example, dogs can assist in child development, helping children to build confidence and aiding cognitive development; some schools get students to read to dogs. More examples of potential benefits are discussed in Chapter 2.

# 2

---

# THE LIFESPAN OF A DOG OWNER

Owning a dog is an integral part of many peoples' lives from childhood through adolescence and adulthood up until older age. Everyone has their reasons for owning a dog but does research support any of those reasons? Can owning a dog truly be a benefit to each and every owner? If so, why doesn't everyone own a dog?

## CHILDHOOD + ADOLESCENCE

In 2003, Gail Melson of Purdue University reviewed the evidence surrounding owning a pet (e.g. dog) and childhood development.

In terms of early life development of thinking skills and how we see the world, it would appear that dogs are intriguing to very young humans. Research has shown that children as young as six months would rather smile at, hold, follow and make sounds towards a pet dog than battery-operated life-like models of cats and dogs. As age progresses, children still prefer to pat and kiss a dog compared to stuffed animals. The stimulation that a 'real dog' gives a child is that of 'predictable unpredictability' which stimulates cognitive curiosity. In addition, when a child is emotionally investing in a situation they are more likely to retain the information and then use it again in different situations. Therefore, owning a dog from a very young age may actually improve the cognitive 'prowess' of children.

In terms of social and emotional development, pet ownership in general is important. Children, when asked to name the ten most important individuals in their lives tend to fill two of those places with their pet dog or other animal! Social support is a significant factor in the physical and psychological lives of children. Many who own dogs between the ages of seven and ten years do gain a great deal of social support from them. For example, children who own dogs are more likely to talk to them about being sad, happy and angry plus secrets than their siblings or parents. Children also tend to mention their pet (e.g. dog) when asked directly who would they turn to, to talk about their emotions. It is then not surprising that children who own dogs and other animals develop nurturance skills quickly once they realise that a dog needs to be cared for throughout its life.

In terms of physical health, a lot of people believe that dog owners, irrespective of age, will be 'fitter and healthier' as they have to walk their dogs on a daily basis. Later on in this chapter we will see if this is true for adults, but is this argument supported by research using children as participants? Carri Westgarth and colleagues from the University of Liverpool in 2016 examined if there was an association between dog ownership and fitness in children. This was one of the first studies to examine this link in children. A sample of over 1,000 children from 31 schools who were attending a SportsLinx Fitness Fun Day completed a Child Lifestyle and Pets Questionnaire. Alongside this, height and weight measures were taken and all children participated in a fitness test (which was part of their SportsLinx day anyway). Contrary to the popular belief surrounding the health benefits of walking a dog, those who owned a dog were equal in fitness status to those who did not own a dog currently. Therefore, the research team were left to conclude that the activity of walking a dog is not sufficient enough to have a direct impact on fitness levels in children.

However, a study published in 2010 by Christopher Owen as part of the Child Heart and Health Study in England did find some impact of dog ownership on physical activity. In a sample of over 2,000 nine- and ten-year-olds, children who had a family dog spent more time in light to vigorous physical activities, had higher levels of activity counts and registered more steps than non-dog-owning children. The research team were quick to note that the results could be *either* a direct influence of having a dog *or* that more active people choose to own dogs so more research is needed to be able to show which of these is true.

## IS THERE A DARKER SIDE TO DOG OWNERSHIP IN CHILDHOOD?

For many years there has been a 'Progression or Graduation Hypothesis' being tested attempting to link negative aspects of dog ownership exhibited by children and subsequent adolescent and adulthood behaviours. This hypothesis states that children who abuse animals such as dogs, 'progress' or 'graduate' to aggression against humans when they are older. Therefore, does evidence of children being cruel to dogs and other animals link in any way to criminal behaviours in adulthood?

Suzanne Tallichet from Morehead State University and Christopher Hensley from the University of Tennessee in 2009 conducted one of the first direct tests of this potential link. A sample of 216 inmates across three prisons completed a questionnaire. This contained a range of questions about childhood animal cruelty and adulthood criminal activities. Extra questions were asked about whether they had hurt animals (including dogs) alone, if they had attempted to cover up any cruelty they had been involved with in childhood and whether the cruelty had upset them. Data was also collected on how many acts of cruelty they had engaged in and how old they were when they first started. It was revealed from the analyses that the only strong predictor of later adult violence-related behaviour was if the act(s) of animal cruelty had been concealed in childhood above any other factor. Therefore, it would appear that those who engaged in acts of animal- (including dog-) related cruelty and were never 'found out' or told anyone were most likely to show multiple acts of violence in adulthood.

Prior to this study, Bill Henry and Cheryl Sanders from the Metropolitan State College of Denver, in 2007, researched if there was a connection between animal abuse and bullying. They investigated a sample of 185 male students aged 18 to 48 years. They completed surveys about their experiences with animals (including dogs), participation in animal abuse (including frequency of), attitudes towards the treatment of animals and experiences as a bully/victim. Overall, those who had experienced high levels of physical bullying but also engaged in high levels of physical bullying were the males who had participated in numerous acts of animal/dog cruelty. The same group also showed the lowest levels of sensitivity attitudes towards animal cruelty. However, it should be noted that the same variables did not link to males who only participated once in an act of animal cruelty. This highlights the need for parents/caregivers to keep a careful eye on how their children interact with their pet dogs at home as any signs of abuse may be indicators of bullying either as a victim or perpetrator.

## *ADULTHOOD*

Previously we had seen how children who owned dogs and walked them did not show increased health on a variety of measures. However, is the same true for adults?

In 2009, Koichiro Oka and Ai Shibata from Waseda University in Japan tested out whether dog ownership is linked to health-related physical activity in Japanese adults. The research used over 5,000 participants with a range of questionnaires completed online. These included a short questionnaire about physical activity, questions about pet ownership (to establish type of pet(s) owned) and a range of demographics were recorded (e.g. gender, marital status, income). From the physical activity questionnaire, the researchers could see estimates of moderate/vigorous physical activity, amount of walking engaged in and sedentary behaviour. The results were as follows:

- Dog owners had larger amounts of moderate/vigorous physical activity compared to owners of other animals and current non-pet owners
- For both amount of walking engaged in and sedentary behaviour, dog owners showed more favourable data compared to the non-pet owners
- Dog owners were 1.5 times more likely to meet the minimum physical activity recommendations in Japan

Therefore, these results are different to those where children are participants. It would appear that owning a dog brings about beneficial health behaviours in adulthood.

## OLDER AGE

A great deal of early research into the human-dog ownership bond and potential health benefits did focus on older adults as participants. However, these tended to be the effects of dogs in care homes and residential settings where the older adults were not having to deal with any of the day-to-day activities that dog owners in their own homes would have to (e.g. walking the dog, vet visits, feeding, cleaning up). However, there are benefits too such as companionship and relief from loneliness. When research began to look at dog owners who were choosing to own the dog (sometimes referred to as community-dwellers) the results became mixed. My own large-scale research which I presented at conferences in Switzerland, the Czech Republic and Scotland clearly showed differences between owners and non-pet owners on a range of psychological and physical health measures such as loneliness, general health and depression. However, when more comprehensive analysis took place that examined how a range of factors (including pet ownership status but also demographics like gender, marital status and age alongside aspects like level of social support) affected physical and psychological health, a different result emerged: owning a dog does have benefits for older adults but only under certain circumstances. For example, older adults living alone with little social contact from friends or family benefit immensely from dog ownership especially in terms of loneliness. However, if a solid human social network is evident then dog ownership only has a minimal impact.

Roland Thorpe and a group of researchers in the United States who formed the Health, Aging and Body Composition Study Group examined something we have already looked at in childhood and adulthood: dog ownership and walking behaviour. They examined over 2,500 older adults (aged 71 to 82) over 36 months. A series of measures were taken including walking behaviour, mobility, health variables and demographics. A range of results emerged:

• Dog walkers were much more likely to reach the recommended 150 minutes of walking per week than dog owners who did not walk their dog(s)
• This was also true for dog walkers and non-dog owners who walked at least three times per week
• Dog walkers tended to show faster 'usual' and 'rapid' walking speeds
• Three years later, the dog walkers were around two times more likely to meet the 150 minutes per week recommendation compared to the rest of the sample

Therefore, it would appear that those who own a dog and walk it manage to keep mobile and walk for longer than those who do not own a dog or own a dog and they do not walk it. This could have implications for older adults to increase their mobility levels: dog-walking groups!

This interaction between owning a dog and actually walking it as a benefit physically was mirrored by Kimberlee Gretebeck in 2013 from the University of Wisconsin. Over 1,000 adults completed measures of physical activity, physical functioning of dog ownership status. Their results complemented those of Thorpe: dog owners who walk their dogs revealed more walking time, more walks, increased physical activity and functional ability. Hence it would appear that having the 'pet obligation' of walking a dog has great benefits for older adults that is not really seen in dog owners who are young.

Could there be psychological benefits of dog walking in older adults? So far we have examined the role of dog walking on physical activity. However, does walking a dog initiate human social contact/support when you meet other people who are out walking too? Early research in this field was done by John Rogers at the University of California. Dog owners were asked to take two walks: one with their dog and one alone. Transcriptions of all conversations were analysed. The majority of content in conversations when dogs were present was the owner instructing the dog or talking about the dogs' wishes and needs. Those passing by would frequently talk about the dog even when it was not present. When the dog owners conversed they often talked about the present whereas non-dog owners talked more about the past. Part of the sample also completed a series of measures for well-being. Current dog owners showed significantly more satisfaction with their physical, emotional and social well-being. Could this be due to simply going out walking with a dog and engaging in casual conversations? It would appear that this could be the case.

Finally, in 2008 Sarah Knight and Victoria Edwards from the University of Portsmouth examined if there were any physical, social and/or psychological benefits of dog ownership in older age. They conducted focus groups (ten in total) to examine if dog owners had similar beliefs about the potential benefits of owning a dog. The average age of the participants was 60 years. There was a 3:1 ratio of females to males. Over 80% had owned dogs all of their lives. Once all of the transcripts had been analysed, there were some common themes associated with the perceived benefits of owning a dog. These included:

- Perceived physical benefits: All participants stated that owning a dog was good for their health via walking

- Perceived psychological benefits: These included giving companionship, comfort and unconditional love
- Dogs as a family member: The status given to a dog matched other people within a family network
- Dogs as therapists: Examples included talking to their dogs about problems and then feeling comforted
- Dogs as providers of safety, security and protection
- Social benefits of interacting because of their dog(s): This included human social interaction when out walking with their dog as it is with like-minded people

## AGE-FREE EVIDENCE

By age-free evidence we mean studies that have used a sample of participants across a wide age group so we cannot specifically pinpoint it to a lifespan developmental phase (e.g. adolescence).

One study that examined the role of dog ownership in depression was conducted by Krista Cline from the University of Missouri and published in 2010. She examined a sample of 201 participants to see if dog ownership played a role in reducing depressive feelings. Participants were aged 19 to 94 years. They completed a battery of questionnaires to measure:

- Depression
- Dog ownership status
- Satisfaction with human social support
- Physical activity
- Demographics

Whilst she reported that dog ownership by itself did not directly affect depression, she did find the following:

1 The relationship between owning a dog and depression had nothing to do with the level of human social support a person was having

2 The same was true for physical activity

3 There was an interaction effect between dog ownership and marital status. That is, the beneficial effects of owning a dog on depression are far greater for single individuals than those who are married.

4 The same interaction was seen for dog ownership and 'sex'. The positive effects were greater for females over males.

Therefore, it would appear that dogs do aid depression in females who are single the greatest.

A common avenue of research as can be seen from this chapter is whether owning a dog means you walk more as a result of that ownership. Shane Brown and Ryan Rhodes from the University of Victoria in Canada examined this link using a wide range age sample in 2006. A random sample of men and women aged 20 to 80 years completed questionnaires about leisure-time walking, general physical activity, dog ownership (including their obligations as a dog owner) and demographics. The main results were:

- Dog owners spent more time in mild to moderate physical activities compared to non-dog owners
- Dog owners walked for an average of 300 minutes per week compared to 168 minutes for non-dog owners
- Dog owners who felt more obligation to undertake things like walking the dog, unsurprisingly, walked more often

They concluded that for those who are willing to take on the responsibility of dog ownership, this could be a 'viable strategy' for increasing physical activity in people who, for physical and psychological reasons, ought to.

Finally, are there dog and/or owner characteristics that could affect the dog-owner relationship? Iben Meyer and Björn Forkman from the University of Copenhagen in 2014 tested out this idea. Over 420

Danish dog owners completed an online questionnaire which consisted of two parts:

1 General questions about themselves and their dog(s)
2 The Monash Dog Owner Relationship Scale (MDORS) which allows a cost-benefit analysis to be made of the dog-owner relationship

All of the participants had previously taken part in the Danish Dog Mentality Assessment (DDMA). The results from the online questionnaire could then be matched with each dog that took part in the DDMA.

Using a statistical technique to group similar behaviours seen in the dogs, a total of five 'dog personality traits' emerged:

- Chase proneness: This involves the dog following and grabbing
- Non-social fear: This involves behaviours like avoiding the sudden appearance of objects and being startled by a metallic noise
- Playfulness: This involves the dog grabbing and playing tug-of-war
- Social fear: This involves behaviours like avoidance and aggression
- Sociability: This involves a set greeting reaction, being co-operative and being handled with no problems

The only 'dog personality trait' to have an effect on the MDORS scores was social fear. That is, if the dog showed this trait in the DDMA tests then the owner was *more likely* to feel *more emotionally close* to that dog. No other 'dog personality trait' predicted MDORS scores. However, when owner characteristics were examined, two main factors emerged:

1 Dog owners who *did not* have children were *more* emotionally close to their dog(s)

2 If the dog is only perceived as being *company* (rather than, say, being an integral part of the family), then that owner was *less* emotionally close to their dog(s)

Therefore, it would appear that different owner and dog traits can affect the emotional bond between dog and owner. More research would be welcomed in this area to try to uncover other dog- and owner-related variables that have an impact on the beneficial nature of the dog-owner relationship.

## THEORIES OF 'HEALTH' BENEFITS

There has been a long-standing argument within the research community as to why there could be benefits for owning a dog. There are three main schools of thought:

1 There is a direct effect of dog ownership on health. That is, owning a dog directly benefits your physical and psychological health.
2 There is an indirect effect of dog ownership on health. That is, owning a dog increases a person's contact with other people and this in turn benefits your physical and psychological health. For example, going out on family walks with the dog or communicating with children whilst out walking.
3 There is a non-causal association between dog ownership and health. That is, factors like your age, personality or health status have an impact on your decision to own a dog which then produces a 'fake link' between dog ownership and physical and psychological health.

Therefore, when reading research about dog ownership and potential physical and psychological health benefits, try to work out which of the three competing theories is being best supported by the study's findings.

## 'SERVICE' DOGS

Dogs have been used for a variety of 'therapeutic' reasons for many years. These have been from Animal Assisted Therapy Dogs in hospitals/ care homes to Guide Dogs for the Blind and Drug Detection Dogs to helping with Bomb Detection. A debate about the welfare issues surrounding these is beyond the scope of this book. Instead, let's focus our attention on two contemporary uses of dogs: to detect diabetes and to detect cancer.

## DIABETES ALERT DOGS (DADS)

In 2013, Nicola Rooney and colleagues published a study claiming that 'trained glycaemia alert dogs' could help people with Type I Diabetes. A total of 19 participants were used in the study. Eleven had a fully trained and certified 'Medical Detection Dog' whilst the other eight had advanced trainee dogs. This training involved scent detection and rewards. All participants were interviewed for approximately 90 minutes so that information could be collected about retrospective examples of experiences with their DADs. The 17 people who completed the study noted that the dogs alerted them to high and low blood sugar levels (this was owner-recorded data). Eight of the ten dogs in the sample that completed the entire study were reported to alert consistently more often when blood sugar was outside the target range for each participant. However, in this study the alert behaviour was not revealed so we don't know if the 'owners' were responding to mere social contact or a specified behaviour. In addition, there was no measure of social support that the dog was giving. Could it be that the diabetic patients were getting some kind of 'new' support which made them more vigilant? As there was no comparison group, we don't know whether just 'being in the study' led to an expectation that 'things will get better' and the patients became better at monitoring their diabetes.

Also in 2013, Ky Dehlinger and colleagues from various medical establishments in Portland, Oregon, USA, used three dogs that had already been 'trained' to respond to hypoglycaemia in their owners. Therefore, they were chosen to see if they could detect 'hypoglycaemic scent' in three people with Type I Diabetes that the dogs did not know. The dogs had already been trained to press a bell after detecting hypoglycaemia. The three human participants took swabs using sterile cotton swabs from both arms – twice when hypoglycaemic and twice when not. The investigators allowed each dog to sniff the samples for 30–45 seconds. Percentage correct detection rates are shown in Table 2.1.

Table 2.1

|  | Dog 1 | Dog 2 | Dog 3 |
| --- | --- | --- | --- |
| % correctly identified swabs | 54.2% | 58.3% | 50.0% |

Source: Dehlinger *et al.*, (2013) Can Trained Dogs Detect a Hypoglycemic Scent in Patients with Type 1 Diabetes? *Diabetes Care*, Vol 36, p. e98–e99

Therefore, it would seem that the three dogs were not that effective at detecting hypoglycaemic patients. Admittedly, the sample size was very small consisting of three patients and three dogs but the dogs had been chosen due to their 'already known ability to detect' which never really transpired in a scientific setting. The researchers note that behavioural cues were not addressed in this study and would need looking at before questioning whether we could use dogs to detect diabetes. These cues may include a person acting differently when hypoglycaemic and it is this, rather than any scent detection, that alerts the dog to a potential problem.

In 2017, Linda Gonder-Frederick and her colleagues at the Behavioural Medical Center at the University of Virginia, USA, conducted a more controlled trial to test the effectiveness of DADs. There had been continued positive reports by diabetes patients that DADs were very useful in a home setting to help them detect when blood glucose levels were either too low or too high. In this study, there were 14 participants who had owned a DAD for at least six months (all were Labrador Retrievers). Over several weeks each participant completed the following:

- Used a glucose monitoring device continuously
- Noted any 'alerts' that their DAD showed

Table 2.2

|  | Awake Low blood glucose | Awake High blood glucose | Asleep Low blood glucose | Asleep High blood glucose |
|---|---|---|---|---|
| % sensitivity score | 35.9% | 26.2% | 22.2% | 8.4% |

Source: Gonder-Frederick, L.A., Grabman, J.H. & Shepard, J.A. (2017) Diabetes Alert Dogs (DADs): An assessment of accuracy & implications. *Diabetes Research & Clinical Practice*, 134, p. 121–130.

A sensitivity score was given to each dog that measured their efficiency at detecting both low and high blood glucose levels.

Table 2.2 shows the sensitivity scores for waking and night-time high and low glucose detection in the DAD sample.

Mirroring the findings of Dehlinger, the research team noted that the majority of DADs 'did not demonstrate accurate detection of low and high blood glucose events'. However, there was great variability across the DADs with 3/14 of them performing better than chance in the daytime and 1/11 during sleeping hours. The research team noted that there has to be more systematic studies of DADs to bridge the gap between the relatively poor findings in a controlled setting compared to the main anecdotal accounts noting that DADs appear to be helping diabetes patients on a daily basis.

## CANCER DETECTION

Whilst controlled trials for DADs have not been as encouraging as first thought, research into cancer detection has been.

Early research conducted by Michael McCulloch and his team from the Polish Academy of Sciences in 2006 tested the accuracy of dogs in detecting early- and late-stage lung and breast cancer. They used rewards to train five household dogs to detect, from breath samples, people with either breast or lung cancer. If the dog 'detected' cancer it was trained to lie down or sit next to the sample. Once trained, all dogs were tested using breath samples from cancer patients (and controls) who did not take part in the training phase. Both sensitivity (correct identification of having disease) and specificity (correct identification of not having disease) scores were calculated. Table 2.3 shows these scores.

*Table 2.3*

|  | Lung cancer Sensitivity | Lung cancer Specificity | Breast cancer Sensitivity | Breast cancer Specificity |
|---|---|---|---|---|
| Proportion correct | 0.99 | 0.99 | 0.88 | 0.98 |

*Source:* McCulloch, M. *et al.* (2006) Diagnostic Accuracy of Canine Scent Detection in Early- and Late-Stage Lung and Breast Cancers. *Integrative Cancer Therapies,* Vol 5(1), p. 30–39

The impressive scores were maintained across all stages of cancer within the sample.

Jean-Nicolas Cornu and colleagues from the University of Paris in 2011 trained a Belgian Malinois to detect scent in urine of a sample of men with prostate cancer. The training phase took 24 months to complete. The dog was then tested on its ability to detect prostate cancer in a sample of 66 patients – 33 with cancer and 33 who had negative biopsies. The dog was always presented with six samples with only one being of that from a man with prostate cancer. The other five were randomly selected controls. The dog detected the cancer in 30/33 patients. In addition, one of the 'incorrect classifications' we re-tested for prostate cancer and it was diagnosed. Overall sensitivity and specificity scores were 91%.

Finally, Ehman and colleagues from the University of Stuttgart, Germany, in 2012 were interested in whether there was a 'presence of a detectable marker' for lung cancer in the breath of patients. Electronic detection devices require patients to not smoke and fast before analyses can take place and this can be quite limiting and time-consuming.

Four household dogs were trained to detect lung cancer from breath samples. In the test phase, the dogs were presented with breath samples from either lung cancer patients, Chronic Obtrusive Pulmonary Disease (COPD) patients or health controls. This was for two reasons – maybe in previous studies, dogs were simply detecting differences in breath between 'healthy and not healthy' and, if the dogs could detect differences between two 'unhealthy' groups then maybe there is volatile compound in the breath of lung cancer patients that can be used in early detection screening.

The overall sensitivity score (correct detection of cancer) was 71% whilst the specificity score (correct detection of no cancer) was 93%. This led the research team to conclude that there must be a 'robust and specific' compound that is present in the breath of lung cancer patients that dogs can detect.

Overall, it would appear that when dog owners are asked about the relationship with their dog and what benefits they feel it brings, they can list a lot of reasons. However, when some of these beliefs are tested systematically it may be just that: a belief. So, maybe we need to ask ourselves this: does owning a dog improve our psychological, physical and social well-being wholeheartedly or do psychologically well-adjusted people who are already physically active and have a good social network choose to own a dog? Is this another case of the chicken or egg, or dare we say it, puppy and dog? Read more research and see what you decide.

# 3

---

# *THE DOG'S NEUTICLES!*

When dog owners can understand the subtleties in how their dogs communicate with each other, as well as with themselves as their owner, then this is likely to have a direct enhancement on the dog-owner relationship. Dogs communicate interspecifically (between different species) and intraspecifically (within a species) through auditory (e.g. barking), olfactory (e.g. smelling body parts) and visual cues (e.g. showing teeth).

## *DOGS' SENSES*

Dogs' hearing is said to be their second most developed sense after smell. They are able to hear frequencies that are well above our listening abilities, for example, ultrasounds. The dog whistles that are used give off sounds of 20,000 to 50,000 Hz. A dog's auditory reach is from 10,000 to 50,000 Hz and a human's is from 16,000 to 20,000 Hz. Some dogs do bark for 'no apparent reason' when they hear sounds that their owner cannot. The owner, confused by this reaction, does not know what to do and might try to hush them. The owner may then think the dog is misbehaving when it's completely the opposite, the dog is trying to defend its territory from a foreign presence. It is also believed that the distance from which a dog can hear things is four times farther than humans and the mobility of its ears helps it better register the nature and source. Dogs have in excess of 15 muscles to move their ears to a human's 6. A dog can distinguish noises that for us sound the same, for example, the sound of their owner's car (which they can tell apart from cars of different brands and models) and their owner's whistle. It has been reported that some dogs can predict earthquakes days before they happen. Experts hypothesise that it is due to the detection of high-frequency sounds coming from the earth or soil vibrations.

A dog's sense of smell is said to be better than humans. Some 200 million or so scent receptors make it much more sensitive than the human nose. The longer the dog's nose, the more scent receptors it has and the more sensitive it is to smell. Dogs with the best sense of smell, such as Beagles and Bloodhounds are sometimes called "scenthounds", have long snouts that house a complicated network of tissues, mucus and scent receptors that enable the dog to recognise smells. The dog's wet nose is designed to help it smell better. Its moisture attracts and holds scent molecules, which then can travel up the nostrils. Sniffing helps to stir up scent particles so that the dog can inhale them. The slits at the corners of each nostril, by flaring out, enable more air to circulate around the nostrils and make the scent strong.

Humans are said to have better sight than dogs, especially when it comes to small objects. Dogs, because of the location of their eyes can detect a movement behind them and their field of vision is much broader than ours. The dog also has improved detection of movement, which is where its skill lies in sighting its prey when hunting. The dog's field of vision is very wide depending on the size of its snout and the skull's shape. A human's sight is binocular and forward, while a dog's is laterally. Dogs have night vision since they have a special membrane that allows them to receive light.

## INTRASPECIFIC COMMUNICATION

For dogs to be able to communicate effectively, their intentions need to be behaviourally clear. The typical wolf-like features facilitate the communication of a dog's motivation. For example, the pointed ears give the ability to sign intent. When placed forward it shows confidence and when placed backwards it implies a submissive state (Figure 3.1).

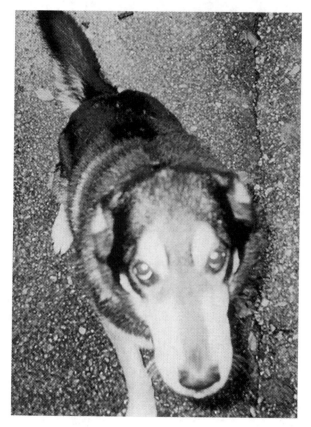

Figure 3.1

The fluffy long coloured tail is an important tool in making a dog's motivations clear. For example, an upright, fluffy tail (and in some breeds these are accompanied with a white tip for additional signing and clarity of intent) implies an aroused and energetic state. Alternatively a tail that is tucked under the back signals submission (Figure 3.2).

Figure 3.2

In those dogs that have been selectively bred to the extreme their ears can be present but functionally redundant. For example, the Basset Hound would find it difficult to use its ears to signal intent.

When these individual behaviours are viewed collectively the dog should be able to demonstrate clearly its entire behavioural repertoire (Figure 3.3 and Figure 3.4) from confident aggression to fear aggression. The dog uses the same behavioural repertoire to communicate

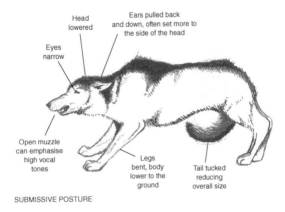

SUBMISSIVE POSTURE

Figure 3.3

Source: Erin Broadbent

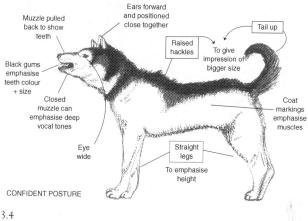

Ears forward and positioned close together

Muzzle pulled back to show teeth

Raised hackles

Tail up

To give impression of bigger size

Black gums emphasise teeth colour + size

Closed muzzle can emphasise deep vocal tones

Coat markings emphasise muscles

Eye wide

Straight legs

To emphasise height

CONFIDENT POSTURE

Figure 3.4

*Source:* Erin Broadbent

with other dogs as it does with humans and this is one suggestion as to why humans and dogs have found it relatively easy to adopt each other's social group.

The extremes of a dog's behavioural repertoire are not usually demonstrated immediately as it shows stages of aggression posturing in order to signal and to avoid wasting energy and overt fighting (demonstrated here in the wolf dog hybrid: Figures 3.5, 3.6, 3.7 and 3.8).

Figure 3.5

Figure 3.6

Figure 3.7

Figure 3.8

## INTERSPECIFIC COMMUNICATION

Given the need for a dog to be physically equipped to communicate effectively, the dog owner may well question their reasons for making breed choices based purely on aesthetics. The contemporary dog owner should place more consideration on to dog welfare than the ability of the dog to communicate when making breed choices. Amicable dog-human associations are formed when there is mutual understanding and a respect of each intention. Whilst dogs are social animals there are some instances where it is not appropriate to apply dog-dog communication and hierarchical systems to the dog-human interactions. A widely overused example of this is the application of "dominance" to control or train unruly puppies. Not only have humans spent thousands of years domesticating and manipulating the dog but also they have equally spent thousands of years observing our behavioural characteristics. Therefore when we behave towards them as another dog would (commonly encountered as dominating the dog) this is contrary to what they'd expect from human behaviour and difficult for them to interpret authentically. For example, confronting a dog that is showing heightened aggressive behaviours and aiming to match or exceed the dog's aggression (humans can do this by shouting or aiming to pin the dog down). This practice is both unethical from an animal welfare viewpoint and irresponsible from a health and safety perspective. As a result their response to this can be unpredictable. Indeed when dog owners contact Behaviour Consultants their main cause of complaint is that their dog is behaving in a way that is unexpected and unpredictable. On visiting dog owners and observing them communicate with their dog, Behaviour Consultants often find that the degree to which people underestimate the ability of their dog to pick up on behaviour is surprising.

## SELECTIVE BREEDING AND DOG COMMUNICATION

In order to appreciate authentic dog behaviour, the dog needs to be able to communicate effectively and natural selection has enabled the canine to do so. However, through selective breeding we have manipulated the gene pool for mainly aesthetic reasons. In many cases this will not only have had an effect on the ability of a dog to communicate but in many cases it can also lead to welfare problems for the dogs themselves.

### Example 1: Bulldog

Physical disadvantage: Prone to respiratory problems due to condensed nasal anatomy and therefore excessive skin around snout

Behavioural complication: More difficult to pull back entire skin around top teeth to imply arousal and/or aggression

### Example 2: Dachshund

Physical disadvantage: Prone to spinal and back injuries due to elongated structure of their spinal column

Behavioural complication: Difficultly jumping up, therefore more difficult to show excitability

### Example 3: Cocker Spaniel (or dogs with floppy ears)

Physical disadvantage: Prone to ear infections

Behavioural complication: Difficultly moving large ears to signal confidence or submission and therefore potentially less likely to be able to exit an escalating interaction with another dog

There are also anecdotal reports of people applying cosmetic procedures for dogs such as silicon implants in testicular sacs when dogs have been neutered in order to stop male dogs experiencing any psychological damage as a result of an aesthetic loss. This can be an obvious source of confusion for dogs when they have the physical cues of being intact and yet none of the scent or secondary behavioural characteristics that align to having testicles.

# 4

---

# THE DOG WHISPERING FALLACY

There are many ways in which any animal can learn new behaviours or adapt existing ones. By understanding how a dog learns it can be seen that this is a more clear-cut process than one which involves "whispering". A movement called 'Behaviourism' in psychology believed that all organisms *learn* in the same ways. Therefore, a wide range of species were used to test out their ideas from pigeons to cats to rats and dogs. The two main ideas are called Classical Conditioning and Operant Conditioning. In both of these the *learner* is quite active in the process. A third idea called Social Learning sees the *learner* as more passive in their role in terms of them not being directly involved in the mechanisms of learning.

## CLASSICAL CONDITIONING – WHAT IS IT?

It is all about learning through association. It is a form of conditioning where the organism (be it human or animal) associates an **unconditional stimulus** with a **neutral stimulus**. After repeated associations, the organism then responds to the neutral stimulus (now called a **conditioned stimulus**) without having the **unconditional stimulus** present anymore.

Ivan Pavlov brought to us the idea of classical conditioning. However, his research was not on humans – he used dogs in this experiments. He was researching digestion in dogs and noticed how some of the dogs reacted to seeing the people who fed them (e.g. barking) before they were given food or just as the person happened to be walking by! He believed that the dogs had **associated** the person with food. Pavlov created a simple experiment to show that his ideas were correct.

Pavlov already knew that dogs would salivate when they smell meat powder. Every time the powder was given to the dogs he sounded a metronome (a device that clicks at set intervals). He repeated this a few times. Then, he sounded the metronome without the meat powder and noticed that each dog salivated. He had successfully classically conditioned the dogs. Figure 4.1 is a diagram highlighting what Pavlov did.

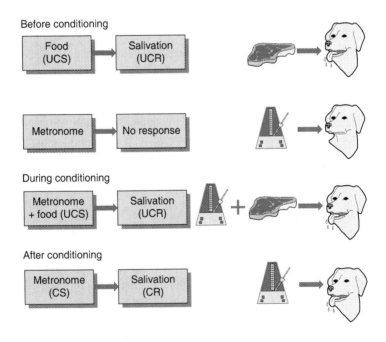

Figure 4.1  Classical conditioning

This type of learnt behaviour can easily be seen in your dog. For example, you may keep dog food in the same cupboard. Have you ever experienced your dog approaching you for food when you open the cupboard even though you had no intention of feeding them? Your dog's behaviour can easily be explained through Classical Conditioning. Look back at the diagram of the Pavlov experiment. Simply replace the 'metronome' with 'opening cupboard' and 'meat powder' with 'dog food'. You may not have known it but you have classically conditioned your dog (and probably without knowing).

## OTHER IMPORTANT TERMS LINKED TO CLASSICAL CONDITIONING

**Generalisation:** This occurs when we produce a conditioned response to a stimulus that is *similar* but not the same as the conditioned stimulus. For example, a dog may produce a fear response to wasps. The dog could *generalise* this fear to other flying insects like bees and hornets!

**Extinction:** This occurs when the conditioned stimulus no longer produces the conditioned response. This could be because the conditioned stimulus has no longer been paired with the unconditional stimulus. So, for example, with the dog fearing wasps, over time the conditioned response of fear disappears in the presence of the conditioned stimulus of the wasp.

**Spontaneous Recovery:** This occurs after extinction. Suddenly, in the presence of the conditioned stimulus the conditioned response re-appears. Again, using the dog fearing wasps, there could have been many months since extinction happened but one day the dog sees a wasp and suddenly it shows lots of fear again.

A great deal of the time it can be very difficult to assess and pinpoint what the original biological Unconditioned Stimulus-Unconditioned Response link is. This may be because some *higher-order conditioning (sometimes called second-order)* has taken place. This conditioning is when a Conditioned Stimulus then gets associated with a different Neutral Stimulus.

## AN EXAMPLE

A common behaviour that can be seen in dogs is excitement when you shout 'Walkies!' But how can this be? This can be easily explained by higher-order conditioning. Figure 4.2 shows this.

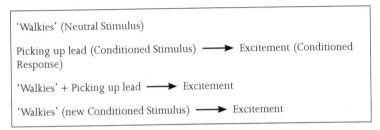

'Walkies' (Neutral Stimulus)

Picking up lead (Conditioned Stimulus) ⟶ Excitement (Conditioned Response)

'Walkies' + Picking up lead ⟶ Excitement

'Walkies' (new Conditioned Stimulus) ⟶ Excitement

Figure 4.2 The previously neutral stimulus of 'Walkies' has become associated with the conditioned stimulus of picking up the lead. Repeated associations will soon make the 'Walkies' a conditioned stimulus all by itself. The dog may then generalise its response to other words that are about the same length and spoken at the same tone as the owner like the dog's name (e.g. Toby) or a name you may have for snacks like 'Treaties!' You have classically conditioned your dog's behaviour.

## OPERANT CONDITIONING – WHAT IS IT?

It is all about learning through consequences. It is a form of conditioning where an organism's behaviour (be it human or animal) is moulded by the use of **reinforcements** (**rewards**) or **punishment**.

Edward Thorndike was one of the first scientists to look into learning by consequence. He had noticed how quickly cats could learn by this technique. He placed a hungry cat in a puzzle box (Figure 4.3) with food outside. The box was set up so that if the cat pulled on a piece of string inside the box, a catch would be released and the door (via a lever press mechanism) would open so the cat could get out and eat the food.

On the first trial, the cat took a long time to escape. The cat moved around the box and *by chance* tugged on the piece of string and released

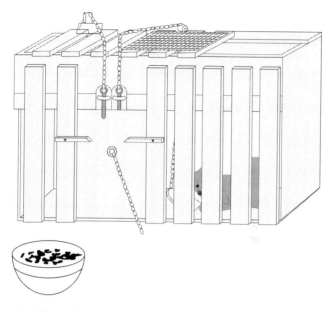

*Figure* 4.3  A Thorndike puzzle box

the catch on the door. Each time the cat was placed back in the box, it escaped more and more quickly. Thorndike believed that the cat had learnt through **trial and error**. From his study he created the **Law of Effect** which states that if behaviour is followed by a pleasurable experience, the organism will be more likely to repeat that behaviour. However, if behaviour is followed by something not so pleasurable then the organism will be less likely to repeat that behaviour.

Burrhus F. Skinner took Thorndike's ideas to a wider audience by introducing a series of terms that are still used to explain how operant conditioning works. The Behaviourist movement was determined to make psychology more scientific and credible so Skinner introduced the concepts of rewards (reinforcements) and punishments as these were more tangible than concepts like pleasure. He felt that aspects of an animal's environment that can be directly manipulated and changed would ultimately explain how an animal both learns a new behaviour and maintains a current behaviour.

They are as follows:

**Positive reinforcement** – the addition of something nice (e.g. reward) that increases the probability of that behaviour being repeated

**Negative reinforcement** – the removal of something aversive that increases the probability of that behaviour being repeated

**Positive punishment** – the addition of something aversive that decreases the probability of that behaviour being repeated

**Negative punishment** – the removal of something nice that decreases the probability of that behaviour being repeated

Table 4.1 shows how to differentiate between the four types of operant conditioning mechanisms

In addition there are two *types* of reinforcement:

1 Primary reinforcer: These fulfil a direct biological need. An example would be a treat for a dog.

*Table* 4.1 Four types of operant conditioning mechanisms

|  | **Positive**<br>This is defined as the addition of something | **Negative**<br>This is defined as the removal of something |
|---|---|---|
| **Reinforcement**<br>This is defined as increasing the probability of repeating the behaviour | **Positive + Reinforcement**<br>This refers to the **addition** of something **nice** to **increase the probability** of that behaviour being repeated | **Negative + Reinforcement**<br>This refers to the **removal** of something **aversive** to **increase the probability** of that behaviour being repeated |
| **Punishment**<br>This is defined as decreasing the probability of repeating the behaviour | **Positive + Punishment**<br>This refers to the **addition** of something **aversive** to **decrease the probability** of that behaviour being repeated | **Negative + Punishment**<br>This refers to the **removal** of something **nice** to **decrease the probability** of that behaviour being repeated |

2 Secondary reinforcer: These have no intrinsic value to the dog but it can be 'exchanged' for a primary reinforcer or it becomes associated with a primary reinforcer. Examples include clicker training (association).

## CAN WE EASILY DIFFERENTIATE REWARDS AND PUNISHMENTS WHEN IT COMES TO DOG BEHAVIOUR?

There can be a fine line between rewarding and punishing dog behaviour. This might appear to be an odd statement as we know when we are rewarding and punishing our own dog. Don't we?

A dog owner can happily talk to their dog to tell them they have done something good like "shake a paw" or "good dog" for sitting in their dog bed. However, the dog may go and set on the sofa and we don't want it. We may say to them "oh, you are a naughty dog, aren't you" and give them a tickle. We think we have punished the dog when in fact we have rewarded that behaviour with attention. Dogs are social species and attention can be a powerful reinforcer of behaviour.

## SOCIAL LEARNING THEORY – WHAT IS IT?

It is all about learning through observation and imitation. For this type of learning mechanism, the actual learner plays a more passive role in the process. They can 'simply' observe others performing behaviours and decide whether to repeat the observed behaviour depending on its witnessed outcome. In other words, you can watch others make mistakes and not have to 'experience them first hand' to learn not to imitate a behaviour. Conversely, you can watch others engaging in positive behaviours and choose to imitate those behaviours even though you still did not 'experience them first hand'.

Basic Social Learning Theory follows four main steps:

1 **Attention.** An observer must pay attention to the behaviour(s) of a role model. This can be someone of higher status, credibility and

as we will see, of a different species! The role model must have some features that are seen as being attractive to the observer. These can be individual factors linked to the role model (e.g. a dog owner) or general traits like being friendly. It had been proposed that same-sex models tend to have more relevant characteristics to the observer.

2 **Retention.** Observers must retain the observed behaviour(s) in their long-term memory. This is so the information can be used again at a later/relevant date and time. This could be when the observer feels they want to imitate the observed behaviour.

3 **Reproduction.** The observer must feel capable of imitating the retained, observed behaviour. If they do, they will attempt to imitate irrespective of the consequences and then refine it to make it more like the observed behaviour or stop imitating if the attempt(s) are not successful.

4 **Motivation.** The observer may experience **vicarious reinforcement** during their observations. This is when the role model is seen to be rewarded for performing the observed behaviour. If this is witnessed then the observer is more likely to want to imitate the behaviour (is motivated) to try and gain the same reward. Also, the observer may experience **vicarious punishment** during their observations. This is when the role model is punished for performing the observed behaviour. If this is witnessed then the observer is less likely to want to imitate.

Overall, this can be seen as 'learning by proxy' as it is initially a product of learning indirectly from others rather than experiencing it 'first hand'.

## IS THERE ANY EVIDENCE THAT DOGS LEARN THROUGH SOCIAL LEARNING THEORY?

Claudia Fugazza and Ádám Miklosi from Eötvös Loránd University in Hungary assessed the 'Do As I Do' method of dog training. Owners had to train their dogs to perform two actions:

1   Open a sliding door. The door was open by 5cm so the dog could paw or muzzle it open.

2   Body movement. A 'jump in the air' action was chosen where the dog was expected to raise at least their front paws off the ground. This was chosen as it was the only novel behaviour in the sample of dogs.

Owners were asked to gain the attention of their dog and show the dog what to do for both actions. Once they had shown the dog they gave a 'Do It!' command. If the dog did not imitate the behaviour, the action was repeated by the owner. Owners were expected to get their dog to repeat the behaviour five times in succession. They were allowed to use rewards but only after they had imitated their behaviour.

More of the dogs who experienced the 'Do As I Do!' method managed to imitate the behaviours in 30 minutes compared to the group that had been clicker trained. Therefore, it would appear that dogs can socially learn through their owners as they must have paid attention to the owner performing the action(s), retained the information, felt capable or reproducing the action and then imitated it.

Examples of types of conditioning can be found in Chapters 5 and 6.

# 5

---

# IS MY DOG ABNORMAL?

Dog owners often ask whether or not their dog is "normal". On one hand dog owners like nothing more than to discuss the quirky behaviour of their pet but often this is balanced with caution in that they are aware there is the potential to be judged. This could be based around the extent other people think that their dog represents an aspect of their own personalities and more so how tolerant they are of their dog's behavioural responses in particular circumstances. The problem is that there are too many variables to consider when asked about a dog "is this normal?" In order to answer the question accurately we would need to consider the following:

- The dog's socialisation experiences
- The environment in which it currently lives
- The dog owner's expectations of their dog's behaviour
- The dog's diet, medical health and physiological limitations which is often the result of selective breeding
- The resources around at the time
- The presence or absence of other people and/or animals
- The environmental factors around leading to the question as to normality

Today, many people keep dogs strictly as companion animals rather than for protection or other functional purposes. As a result there is increased necessity for the behaviour of the dog to be socially acceptable. Misunderstandings occur and there remains a difference between what dog owners consider to be a "behaviour disorder", a "behaviour problem" and an "inappropriate behaviour". Therefore to describe any behaviour as completely normal or completely abnormal is not always straightforward. As a result the psychological terms "typical" and "atypical" can be applied to the description of dog behaviour to include more commonly agreeable behaviours exhibited as part of the domestic dogs' behavioural repertoire. The following definitions can be applied for the terms used in this area:

- **Behaviour disorder** implies a biological or medical aspect to the dog's behaviour
- **Inappropriate behaviour** encompasses all aspects of dog behaviour that is for the owner inappropriately placed and could be a welfare issue for the dog
- **Behaviour problem** appears to be a caveat for all aspects of dog behaviour that could be a welfare issue for the dog and a source of dissatisfaction for the dog owner

It should be noted that within populations of dogs there are some of them that are demonstrating normal dog behaviour patterns that are inappropriately directed and considered acceptable by some owners and unacceptable by others. This might include jumping up, mounting people, enthusiastically smelling people's groins; behaviours directed to other dogs, for example, unsolicited mounting, licking genitals; aggressive behaviours and behaviours directed to the environment such as digging on the lawn, retrieval of food from surfaces, excessive vocalisations and damage to property in the absence of an owner. The majority of experienced dog owners are often very tolerant of innate behaviour exhibited by their dog and owners will often say they are the most rewarding. In the main, atypical dog behaviours are reported only when they appear to be causing the dog distress and/or the owner believes it poses a risk to people or other animals. Such behaviours include separation-related behaviour training problems, phobias, stereotypical and playing-related behaviours.

Separation-related behaviour refers to a particular set of behaviour patterns that occurs exclusively when a dog is left alone. These include destructive chewing, excessive vocalisations, digging, consumption of non-food stuffs, urination and defecation. They also include aggressive behaviour patterns directed towards the owner when leaving their dog. These behaviours can have varied motivations, such as:

- Over-attachment to owners
- Lack of habituation to separation from the members of their social group
- Fear of specific stimuli (such as noises) that generalise to a particular context

Training issues can be defined as any normal dog behaviour patterns that occur inappropriately, or any desired behaviour not readily carried out by the dog on command. Training issues can include loss of toilet training, pulling on the lead and not returning to the owner when the dog is called.

Phobias can be defined as excessive or extreme fear response to a stimulus. Phobic responses often involve whining, panting, shaking, running or hiding in response to a particular event or person. Phobias are often elicited by loud noises but can also result from stimuli such as unfavourable people, insects such as bees or wasps particularly if a dog has had a sting.

Stereotypes are defined as any repetitive behaviour pattern that has no obvious function; for example, tail chasing and fly snapping are common examples. Stereotypical behaviour is often considered as having developed as a coping strategy during chronically stressful situations and is therefore assumed to be a dog welfare issue. Sadly evidence of such behaviour is often shown for entertainment on television and in social media channels which suggests that such anxiety-motivated behaviours are not always considered serious enough to treat with behaviour modification. Indeed the contrary would apply as such behaviours are rewarded which perpetuates the welfare issue for the dog.

Aggressive behaviour can be difficult to define because it is multifactorial in nature. However there are some aspects which are common to all forms of aggression. The purpose of aggressive behaviour is not always to cause pain or destruction to another animal. In the domestic dog these can be direct or indirect towards inanimate objects. Dogs will often use the context of play to practice aggressive behaviours with their intent to not destroy. However, the serious consequences of inappropriate aggression means it is relevant to both the welfare of the dog and public safety, e.g. in 2015 in the USA 82% of dog bite victims were aged less than nine years old and in the UK the youngest registered dog-bite-associated fatality was aged less than a week old.

There are several overlapping types of aggressive behaviour that are recognised as being a cause of concern to the dog owner. These include confident, predatory, territorial, possessive, protective, fear-induced, playing-related, interspecific/intraspecific and learned aggression. Aggression is most often related to fear or confidence and it links to the fight or flight response.

Confident aggression has often been explained by making analogies to theories of dominance relationships. This is not necessarily a sound approach as the function of dominance relationships in social groups is to ensure social stability and actually prevent fighting. In a group of feral dogs the so-called alpha male or dominant dog is predominantly male. However, this status is likely to change depending on the situation and the resources available in a domestic setting. It will also be influenced by the dog's relationships with other species such as humans, felines and other household pets. Therefore it is nonsensical to apply strict rules in a hierarchical structure that is dynamic to one more often seen in wolf packs or wild dogs. A rise in TV programmes about managing dog behaviour correlates to a rise in reports suggesting that it has become a relatively common practice for owners to try and exert dominance over their dog in order to keep it in a submissive state in an attempt to make the dog more agreeable and easier to control. However, in doing so there is the potential for owners to be overzealous in the application of dominance and the outcome is often one where their pet dog becomes fearful and anxious as they perceive their owner to behave in an unpredictable heavy-handed manner.

Predatory aggression is characterised by hunting or stalking postures. It is possible that such aggression is motivated differently from the other types of aggressive behaviours as often there are no warnings given by the dog (as this would assist the prey to escape). This therefore differs significantly from intraspecific forms of aggression where warnings are important in order to *reduce* the chance of aggressive behaviour. Predatory aggression can be directed to any living organism and also has been seen to be directed to inanimate objects.

Territorial aggression is shown when the dog's physical space area is breached and warning signs are often given before an attack. Territorial aggression can occur at home and possibly when out on walks, especially if the dog feels that the owner is part of its own territory and is readily taken to the same area for exercise.

Possessive and protective aggressions tend to occur in situations when a dog feels there is a threat to its resources, for example, its food or access to its owner. Therefore the dog can become protective and may also become aggressive to people that the owner tries to talk to on the street. This type of aggression may be linked to dominance aggression but is more commonly associated with a fear response as a consequence of inconsistent owner behaviour and rewards.

Fear-induced aggression is hallmarked by fearful behaviour patterns (e.g. ear and tail down, snaps and withdraws). This is a typical behavioural response in an animal that feels threatened or unable to escape.

## HOW IS AGGRESSION CLASSIFIED?

Aggression is classified according to behaviour patterns exhibited by the dog. There are other factors that contribute to a presentation of aggression. These include gender, age, selective breeding and medical factors.

Maternal aggression can occur during pregnancy, postpartum or during a false pregnancy (pseudopregnancy). During pseudopregnancy a mother may show aggression to even inanimate objects. Maternal aggression is displayed when the mother is acting to protect her young from a perceived threat at a time when she knows they are vulnerable. The aggressive behaviour of a mother dog at this time has been reported as being misused by abusive dog owners in using postpartum bitches as fighting dogs and baiting them with their own puppies to induce their maximum aggressive behaviour. Freud suggested that aggression is linked to sexual motivation. Indeed fighting in animals can be considered reproductively motivated as the majority of fights involve males of the same species. Generally, males are more aggressive than females and hormonal factors can have an influence on this. Testosterone alone does not cause aggression. It merely acts as a facilitator. More intact males and neutered females are referred to therapy for aggression-related problems. If female dogs are behaving aggressively and they are spayed, they can be more aggressive afterwards. This is because spaying usually occurs at social maturity which is a time when aggressive behaviour would normally start. It has been reported that female mammals when in the womb with other males can become masculinised at birth as a result of hormonal influences and may be more aggressive as a result of this exposure.

Aggressive behaviour normally starts around the time of sexual maturity (6–12 months) in both males and females. During this time aggression can increase or decrease. The lack of socialisation in puppies (up to 16 weeks) may contribute to their being aggressive in later life due to the inadequate development of canine social responses, such as threat and submission.

Factors influencing aggressive behaviour may be transmitted genetically. Genes affecting growth patterns in turn will have an influence on strength and this has been reflected in breed types that were targeted in the Dangerous Dogs Act 1991. There is some disagreement as to whether or not aggressive behaviour is a heritable trait but the field of epigenetics looks at the role of environmental factors on gene expression and how this influences behaviour in animals and humans. The increase in the use of puppy farms led to a larger turnout of unsocialised common breeds due to limited environmental and social experiences that have led to an increase in anxiety, which is often the root cause of aggression in dogs. This suggests aggression cannot be related purely to a breed type, although it has been suggested that selective breeding can be used to increase the characteristics associated with overt aggression required for dogs intended to be used in unethical fighting practices. It is suggested that fighting dogs may have a higher pain tolerance which could be due to changes in brain chemistry or an increase in testosterone levels. Whilst some dog breeds are reported to be more aggressive than others, it should be noted that investigations into breed differences may reflect the most common dog breed in the community. For example, cattle dog breeds were very high on the aggression listing in research that was carried out in Australia where a large number of cattle dogs were to be expected. It is therefore evident that genetics as well as environmental factors will determine the level of aggression exhibited by any individual dog.

Medical conditions can be responsible for the cause of canine aggressive behaviour and there is often a significant overlap with neural and hormone systems. Aggressive behaviours that are due to untreatable medical conditions cannot be treated with behaviour modification, for example, brain tumours and rabies can also cause aggressive behaviour. There is no one biological or psychological system that controls aggression exclusively, and experimental evidence suggests that neural systems exist in the brain for various types of aggression.

Many psychological researchers agree that there is no such thing as an "aggression centre", and factors influencing the intensity of attacks include sensory information, presence of relevant external stimuli and previous experience. There are several hormones and neurotransmitters involved in behaviour and the release of stress hormones such as cortisol. This has been implicated in several studies of animal welfare and is considered a more accurate measure of stress in animals. Once a baseline of cortisol levels is established and paired with a stress-provoking stimulus in the environment, any change in the environment can be correlated with cortisol levels and be an indicator of stress and welfare.

## WHAT IS STRESS?

Stress was originally described as a non-specific response made to any demand on the body. Today the term 'stress' is overused in everyday society. Since the 1930s within the fields of psychology and behaviour, the terms 'eustress' and 'distress' have been used to better illustrate the difference between controllable and uncontrollable stress respectively. However, there appears to be no one universally accepted definition of the different types of stress experienced by all mammals including humans. One of the issues in agreeing on a universal definition is that from a psychological perspective stress can be subjective both between and within different species of mammals. In research, hormonal levels of stress (e.g. cortisol) provide an objective measure as to what the dog is experiencing.

## THE CENTRAL NERVOUS SYSTEM (CNS) AND THE STRESS RESPONSE

The hypothalamus is an important part of the nervous system, which, together with the hormonal system controls the internal state of the body. The hypothalamus controls the release of pituitary hormones which subsequently act as messengers. Carlson 1998 demonstrates that the emotions of rage and aggression are sourced at the hypothalamus although these can be inhibited. Research evidence suggests that if a puppy was not adequately socialised it is possible that connections in the brain are not made between sensory input and the inhibition centres of emotion. As a result the range of neural plasticity and ability to adapt is reduced when the puppy becomes an adult dog.

The stress response begins within the CNS as the perception of threat to homeostasis (the maintenance of an internal equilibrium). As stress is essential to life, this response is not necessarily something to be avoided. However, distress can be considered aversive and it is associated with the emotional response of fear, for example, in the immobilisation of dogs. Prolonged states of stress are detrimental to welfare as a mammal's perceived controllability is important in influencing cortisol release as exposure to stress can cause anxiety.

Animals develop very similar diseases as humans do when they suffer prolonged or uncontrollable stress and this would result in increased blood cortisol. Chronic physiological stress is also recognised by an increase in glucocorticoids (a family of steroid hormones of which cortisol is one).

The dog has paired adrenal glands, situated at the front of the inner side of each kidney. Each gland has two separate hormone-synthesising components produced by the adrenal gland (the outer cortex and an inner medulla). The medulla produces adrenaline (epinephrine), an emergency hormone that prepares the dog physiologically to respond to fight-or-flight situations. The cortex produces steroid hormones in very small quantities that are also essential for the stress response.

The adrenal gland responds to the CNS and sends this information to the hypothalamus which then produces hormones that travel to the pituitary gland and then the adrenals where in the dog the predominant glucocorticoid cortisol is released. The function of the glucocorticoids is to prepare the body for physical activity, for instance, there is a switch from anabolic (building up) to catabolic (breaking down) activity as well as that all non-essential processes are supressed. Both acute and chronic stress divert resources away from essential biological functions which is why too much stress is considered detrimental to welfare. However, due to variations in the domestic environment, it can be difficult to obtain accurate physiological measures of stress and it is therefore beneficial to use such hormonal measures alongside behavioural assessments. This means that we can correlate what a dog is showing (the behaviour) and what a dog is sensing (hormones).

## BACK TO THE BEHAVIOUR

Given the variation in how dogs behave depending on where they are or who they are with, how can we be sure that we are interpreting the correct behaviours and that we are all talking about the same things? Scientifically this has been resolved by measuring dog behaviour against a specialist diagram called an Ethogram (Table 5.1). Such tools assist researchers in providing the same reference point for the identification of dog behaviour patterns.

Without the use of an ethogram baseline, measures of a dog's behaviour cannot be quantified and the degree to which behaviour modification can be valued to change a dog's behaviour cannot be determined.

Against an ethogram, atypical behaviour can be considered as containing behaviour patterns that are the result of inappropriate associated learning, operant conditioning, caused by disease and not part of the dog's typical behavioural repertoire. It is noteworthy that whilst a dog might spin around to lick its bottom, this could be on an ethogram and considered as part of grooming. However, a dog exhibiting that same behaviour repeatedly for several minutes (and in some cases hours or even days on end) would be considered atypical. Dog behaviour can be considered typical but depending on the frequency and the initiating stimuli it could be representative of atypical behaviour patterns and is potentially a welfare issue. Therefore each case is better considered on an individual basis. It is always very important that the first step in considering behavioural change in a dog is one which is determined by a veterinary surgeon. This is in order to rule out ill health that could be remedied by pharmacological intervention.

Table 5.1

| Behaviour | | Description |
|---|---|---|
| Ear Position | Up | Tip of pinna pointing above head |
| | Down | Tip of pinna pointing towards the back of the head |
| Tail Position | Tucked | Tail located between the back legs |
| | Relaxed | Tail limp and hung loosely to the rear of the dog |
| | Flag | Tail upright with the tip facing above the head or slightly curled at the end, may or may not be moving |
| Tail Movement | Moving | Tail in motion in any direction |
| Head Posture | Up | Head raised up above the withers |
| | Level | Head in line with the withers |
| | Down | Head hung below the level of the withers |
| Body Posture | Stand | Body in a stationary upright position with weight distributed between four feet |
| | Sit | Body in an upright position with the dog's weight placed upon the joint of the hind leg between the knee and the fetlock |
| | Lie | Body deposited ventrally or laterally on a surface |
| Movement | Walk | All gaits where at least one foot is in contact with the ground at any one time |
| | Run | Dog moves with speed and smooth motion |
| | Jump | Dog leaps from the ground with a sudden start, either front two, or all four feet leave the ground |
| Proximity | Near Familiar | Dog orientates its head (nose) towards a familiar person, dog or toy |
| | Near Unfamiliar | Dog orientates its head (nose) towards an unfamiliar person, dog or toy |
| Vocalisations | Bark | Sharp explosive cry |
| | Growl | Gutteral murmur of antagonism |
| | Whimper | Crying querulously or to whine softly, can be a high- or soft-pitched vocalisation |
| Elimination | Urinate | Discharge of urine from body |
| | Defecate | Discharge of faeces from body |

Training and/or behaviour modification should not be considered a panacea for all unwanted dog behaviour as it is very important to determine the root cause of any behavioural change. This usually starts with gaining information from the dog owner.

**The following case studies are a work of fiction and based largely on the more common of hundreds of cases seen by Behaviour Consultants over 25 years of education, research and practice. Client and dog names, businesses, places, events, locales and incidents are fictions so any resemblance to actual dogs or persons, living or dead, or actual events is purely coincidental.**

## CASE STUDY 1

Name: Sally
Breed: Miniature Dachshund
Colour: Black and Tan
Gender: Female (spayed)
Age: 2 years

The owner is asked to write about the dog and the issue in their own words: "Sally is VERY ATTACHED to me even though I do everything with her we play a lot and she loves going on to her back and for me to rub her tummy, but she doesn't let Jack (my fiancé) go near her. We both love her and I've only left her alone once (when we first got her I had to change my working hours so I could be in with her) but she was with Jack and they got on fine they went on walks and in fact he saved her from going under a car. We have had her from 6 months and as far as we know she only had one male owner who was a breeder in North Wales but she kept absorbing the puppies so he got rid of her. We got her from a dog charity where she was put in a kennel initially with a Frug (Frenchie Pug cross) and after a while she was put in the charity office by herself – I'm guessing because it was best for her. Me or Jack have never had a dog before but when we got this flat we thought it would be nice to get a dog as we are not planning on having kids for a year or two. But Jack did have 4 cats when he was growing up and I used to breed rabbits and I had a ferret for a short time so we both liked the idea of having a small or toy dog as this would suit our life. The main problem is that she is getting more jealous and scared of him. She barks at him constantly. I play with Sally loads, but Jack doesn't as she really doesn't like him, she did at first but as time has gone on it has just got worse and worse, so Jack doesn't play with her at all, he can't even look at her. Now every time Jack looks at Sally she starts to shake and if he comes in the room she'll go under the table and if he walked over to the table she will do a wee wee. It's always very runny and very difficult to pick up. We took her to the vet to make sure that she was not sick and she said she was fine she even did a blood test and there is nothing wrong with Sally which is why the vet said to contact you. Since we contacted you it has got even worse because Sally has started looking out for Jack's car and she barks as soon as she comes to the front door before he's even got inside. Neighbours have started to complain. When I try to explain how and what has happened I think they think Jack has done something to Sally to make her so nervous of him, but he has done nothing, he can't even get close to her. The other morning Sally was in the kitchen and we were at the front door and Jack came to give me a kiss goodbye and Sally starting growling at him and went under the kitchen counter and did a wee wee and she'd only just come in from the garden. She hates even going out on walks with him now and he hasn't done anything to hurt her I promise you! It's all very upsetting as I don't want to rehome her again. Please can you help us? Victoria"

*Classification: Possessive and/or defensive
and/or fear aggression*

Explanation from the dog's perspective: Sally has most likely had an inadequate socialisation period (poor social learning) in that she is not likely to have had much time in a domestic environment if she was raised on a conventional puppy farm. She may well have had rough handling by her breeder and whilst she was originally comfortable around Jack she will have relearned that men are associated with distressful situations (classical conditioning) when he grabbed her out of the way of a car. Sally may not have perceived the car as a threat and only experienced the rough and spontaneous handling by Jack (operant conditioning/classical conditioning). Sally may also have learnt that the presence of Jack means that she loses her most valued resource (Victoria) as whenever Jack and Victoria are present Sally receives less attention (negative punishment). Sally may have also learned that her behaviour is the correct response as whenever she behaves in this way she gets what she wants, for instance, Jack goes away and she is rewarded with the inevitable reassurance/attention (negative reinforcement as Jack disappears alongside the positive reinforcement of Victoria's attention which is conflicting) from Victoria and therefore Sally learns that this is the correct behavioural response.

## CASE STUDY 2

Name: Ace
Breed: Cairn Terrier
Colour: Wheaten
Gender: Male (neutered)
Age: 4 years

The owner is asked to write about the dog and the issue in their own words: "Ace is the perfect dog, we got him for Christmas and have had him now six months and we could not be happier. He doesn't give any trouble when you take him out for a walk. He always comes back when you call him and he doesn't have a bad bone in his body. When our friends and family come to the house they trust him to play with the kids and I have never even heard him growl – until last week. As the evenings are longer now we thought we'd give him his walks later in the evening as we enjoy walking and as it was a weekend we took him out at around 6pm for a long walk on the beach front. As it got to 7pm and the seasonal summer firework show came on Ace started to go berserk! He was pulling me on the lead, making a funny noise, jumping around as if he was on hot coals, people started turning around to look at me, the wife looked at me agog she didn't know what to do and I wasn't having that and I told him, 'Ace you stop this' (I know you really have to dominate a dog when they mess you around I learnt that in my military days) and I used a big yank on the lead to show him I meant business. So I must admit I was quite surprised when he growled at me at which point I dropped the lead and he ran off over the cliff top, thankfully he went to the road side rather than the cliff edge as he could have been a goner. The car that hit him was driving very slowly so the vet said it could have been a lot worse, but it was just bruises and he is better now. When we were at the vets the surgery advised me on medication for Ace for the 6 Friday nights in the summer when the fireworks are on (and they were the ones who gave me your number). My wife wasn't keen to have Ace medicated so she got some massage oils and herbal pills from her friend who is an actual herbalist. The following Friday when the fireworks came on every time Ace started to show any signs of being nervous my wife gave him a rub which seemed to help him a bit. Last Friday my wife had to go and see her mother who had had a fall so it was just me and Ace so I thought the best thing to do was to throw him in at the deep end so at 6:30pm I took him down and stood at the front of the firework display so he had some time to get used to it and at 7pm when the fire works went off I was ready. Well he was worse than ever, he didn't know what to do with himself, he was jumping up and flipping round I just had to leave. I spoke to my wife about it and we agreed we don't know what to do so I said to my wife we need some help with this and would appreciate anything you can do. Perhaps you can just give us some advice as it looks like he is likely to have one of these bouts again, Wilf"

### Classification: Specific noise anxiety

Explanation from the dog's perspective: Ace is a rescue dog and therefore little would be known about his previous experience. It is possible he would not be not used to an environment with spontaneous noise such as fireworks and he paired the noise with a negative behaviour (noise and the "dominating" behaviour of Wilf; classical conditioning) from his owner who would have unwittingly made Ace feel that his growling response was appropriate. When the stimulus appeared again in the form of fireworks the following week, Ace would have made an association that the outcome would be the same and he anticipated such a confrontation by preparing for it as demonstrated by his anxiety (classical conditioning). Wilf's wife also rewarded this anxiety as Ace received attention for his display of fear therefore unwittingly rewarding (positive reinforcement) his inappropriate behaviour.

## CASE STUDY 3

Name: Deontay
Breed: Rottweiler
Colour: Black
Gender: Male (unneutered)
Age: 3 years

The owner is asked to write about the dog and the issue in their own words: "Deontay is really stressing out my Mum as he's not keen on her. I've not had him to myself for long but since my mum comes around every day to help me with the kids (I have got a little girl who is going to school next month and a little boy who is the same age as Deontay) he's been a bit naughty. For a start he poos in the house, he always does his wees outside but once we were all in the garden and he's come inside to do a poo. I didn't tell him off or anything but he got grumpy when my mum who shouted to him to come out, and she forced his head down to rub his nose in it but because he's so big and she had her hands full (holding my little boy at the time) she just got the poo everywhere. He still poos inside now. I think that's why he doesn't like her as after that he'd always go up to her when she walks around. If she's sitting on the sofa then it's fine but as soon as she reaches out to one of the kids he goes right up to her face and growls so deeply I can feel it vibrating. So she is now worried and I've noticed that she's not coming around much anymore. She says it's because when we all sit in the front room she has to sit on the floor (it's quite a small front room) but she never minded before and that's when my boyfriend was living here too. Deontay is my dog but he isn't completely, my boyfriend worked nights as a security at this car breakers yard and so before we had my little girl we both wanted a dog and my friends Rotty had puppies so it was two birds with one stone. My boyfriend takes Deontay to work with him at night and I could have him for company in the day when my boyfriend was asleep. But he's left me with the kids now and it's not that I didn't want him to leave Deontay I just didn't think I'd have the dog to walk as well as the kids, and now my mum can't help. I tried tying him on to the buggy when I walk the kids but he just pulls so much and I'm not strong enough to control him. So yesterday when it all kicked off I actually hadn't walked him all week as I was so busy with the kids so I think he was full of energy. My mum came round yesterday and I must admit we had a bit of a go at each other because I was saying how I needed her to at least come around and watch the kids so I could try to take Deontay around the block for a walk and she started shouting at me and said she'd take the kids out herself. Deontay then just started walking round and round, not to his meet his own bum, but he kept nudging the kids and putting them together and walking in a circle round and round and round the kids. Sometimes I think the kids think they are his puppies the way he carries on, they are just oblivious to it. But then my mum reached over to pick up my little boy and Deontay did that growling and showed her literally all his front teeth. I've never seen him do that before. So she stepped back and his face immediately went back to normal, it was so weird, he just carried on circling the kids so I went to pick up my little boy and Deontay didn't do anything. But seeing me do that my mum went to pick up my little girl and he got really cross. I've never seen the hairs on his back go up before but my mum went very pale and told me she can't help me as long as I have the dog. I'm not sure what to do about it really I love him very much, he's like having one of my own kids, but I just can't carry on like this, Bella"

*Classification: Protective aggression and territorial behaviour*

Explanation from the dog's perspective: Deontay had learnt that the shepherding of the children is an appropriate behaviour and it is likely that he has been rewarded (positively reinforced). This was done via the verbal praise as part of his training, although done with good intention from his male owner it was irresponsible given the health and safety considerations and risks to the children. This is particularly concerning given the size difference, space restriction in the home and the obvious potential for misunderstandings to occur. Deontay demonstrated protective behaviour of the children and it is possible that he interpreted Bella's mum to be a threat to the children as a result of her behaving overly aggressively towards him whilst holding the little boy and behaved with a degree of protective aggression.

## CASE STUDY 4

Name: Unknown
Breed: Unknown
Colour: Tan
Gender: Males (unneutered)
Age: Unknown

The owner is asked to write about the dog and the issue in their own words: "We have had always taken on our charitable responsibilities extremely seriously. Even when were on holiday in Spain we like to go around the dog shelters to give donations to the ones we think need the most help. We really like helping EXPATPETS (INTERNATIONAL) as we know they are really committed, they run a really tidy shelter and the dogs generally look in terrific condition. The long and short of it is that we met these two brothers, they were strays, scrawny as anything but absolutely huge, their paws were literally the size of my hand and they were similar to the ones we glimpsed when we travelled the Northern Rockies but even in their poor condition they looked so unintimidated, the kind of dog that wouldn't look out of place on Game of Thrones. To say we fell in love with these dogs is an underestimation, my partner said there was no way we were leaving Spain without owning them. So we put the paperwork in place before we left. We knew XPATPET would look after them and get them into good condition and we went home to prepare for them. We told everyone about them, put pictures on our social media and have had so much interest in them. All our friends are dog lovers and my partner's sister who does wildlife photography asked to do a photo shoot with them in the New Forest. We have now had them home four days and we haven't even given them names (as we thought we'd see what their personalities are like first) but things aren't going well. We realised that we don't have any history for these dogs, we don't even know how old they are so we took them to our local vet to register them and the vet had to come out to our campervan to see the dogs (as we realised that they were too bulky and agile so we couldn't get a lead on them). The vet was concerned more about how their behaviour might develop as they had been given all their checks and vaccines in Spain so she suggested that we contact you. The problem is they only seem to have eyes for each other, the first day we gave them the run of the house, so they could get used to our home and they spent most of the time in our bed and in the garden. The second day it was obvious we had underestimated how much they'd eat as there is literally no filling them. In one sitting they had six chicken breasts between them and then got irritated when

I put the rest away. So, by yesterday we thought they'd have had enough time to settle and we invited my partner's sister (the photographer) and her friend round, we did what we were told about reintroductions. We sat the visitors down and then let the dogs in. It was awful the girls were sitting on the sofa and the dogs just ran in barking and growling, they looked completely different, they looked even bigger than before. It was extraordinary how their tails got so high, their ears were pointed all the hairs were up on their backs, their teeth were on show as they ran in without even looking at us straight up to the girls, (it was as if they had agreed they'd have one each), well my partner's sister jumped up and turned around and the dog just quickly bit the back of her thigh and her friend put her hand out so she was bitten very badly on the side of the hand. What was so strange is that even though we were shouting, the dogs just kept going at the girls and they made multiple bites, they just would not relent. It's lucky that me and my partner are so strong as it was a job just to pull them off the girls and we actually both got bitten in the process (my partner was marked on his face). It was honestly the worst experience of my life, we were all shaking. There was blood on the sofa and carpet, and we have left them in the garden. Last night we put food out in the kitchen and then left the back door open so they can come into the kitchen for shelter. Today they are behaving as if nothing has happened. We felt so bad for the girls and now we don't know how to cope with the dogs. We really need some help, Eric"

### Classification: Confident aggression/territorial aggression

Explanation from the dog's perspective: The confident aggression shown by both these dogs would imply that they have learnt that indiscriminate aggression to this extent is required in the majority of circumstances in which they are present. The most unassuming explanation is that the dogs have learnt that when they behave in this way they get the outcome they want, most likely to be in the case of feral dogs that the threatening person goes away (negative reinforcement). This is likely if the dogs perceived the girls as threat. As explained Chapter 1 the causes of aggression are multifactorial and therefore it would be nonsensical to speculate as to the specific cause.

# 6

---

# TREATING AND PREVENTING ABNORMAL DOG BEHAVIOUR

How can psychological learning theory help the treatment of atypical behaviour? If a dog has learnt to behave in a particular way in order to obtain a reward, we can change how often we give that reward to manipulate the dog's behaviour. From a psychological perspective there are many different methods to use:

**Desensitisation** is the process by which an association is weakened and the dog becomes less behaviourally reactive due to the gradual exposure to the stimulus previously enlisting the undesirable behavioural response. *For example, in case study 1 Sally needs to be desensitised to the presence of Jack.*

**Counter-conditioning** is the method by which an animal is taught an alternative behaviour that is incompatible to the previous undesirable behaviour. *For example, in case study 1 once Sally is desensitised she needs counter-conditioning and subsequent reward for any voluntary interaction (not matter how mild) with Jack.*

**Extinction** refers to a decrease of a behaviour pattern over time due to the withdrawal of all forms of reinforcement (reward).

**Habituation** involves repeated presentation of a stimulus until the stimulus no longer results in a response. The stimulus has to have been a novel one.

**Rewards** from a social dog perspective means any form of attention (including food) becomes an acknowledgement of behaviour e.g. any verbal, physical attention to include eye contact in all cases. These can then increase the probability of the dog repeating a desirable behaviour.

**Flooding** is exposing the organism to the most fearful situation immediately and without any real escape. For example, in case study 2 Wilf taking Ace to all of the firework show which was not a good idea and is a welfare issue.

## THE USE OF REWARDS AND PUNISHMENT

A responsible Animal Behaviour Consultant will advise the use of positive reinforcement techniques in behaviour modification as using punishment techniques can cause anxiety and has been found to be counterproductive in training dogs as well as being a potential welfare issue. For example, in case study 3 Bella's mum rubbing Deontay's nose in his faeces. Punishments include physical as well as vocal reprimands, booby traps, spontaneous noise (including shouting), water squirting, choke collars/chains and electric or citronella collars. If a dog is motivated to perform a behaviour pattern and subsequently punished for doing so, then although the dog may not show that behaviour pattern again it may still remain motivated to do so but feel anxious about what will happen if it does. Therefore it is always more useful to address/manage that motivation for that behaviour and cause change through reward-based behaviour modification.

In all cases the dogs need checking by a veterinary surgeon for signs of ill health and charitable animal welfare societies can provide reduced costs in means-tested households. Owners should be aware of any pain that may develop and the possibility of dogs behaving innately defensive. All dogs should be covered with the appropriate insurances (which will often cover the costs of a behavioural consultation should you go to a registered Behaviour Consultant). There is rarely a case when there is one single issue involved in atypical dog behaviour. Non-confrontational behaviour modification programmes are effective in manipulating most unwanted dog behaviour directed to owners. These secondary treatments include the following.

## ENRICHMENT TECHNIQUES

Enrichment refers to anything that enhances a dog's situation by giving them things to occupy them that are independently rewarding. These devices include chewing or dog food delivery devices, hollow bones with treats stuffed in, purchasable devices that the dog pushes and rolls for intermittent food delivery. Enrichment devices will provide mental stimulation and include a range of apparatus in the form of toys and treats that will keep them occupied and rewarded. There are several of these on the market. The dog is then independently self-rewarded rather than needing to make contact with their owner for rewards in the form of physical attention. For both anxious and confident dogs this can help them to relax and alter their focus respectively. Some owners choose to purchase a food delivery device and make their dogs work for all their food but the appropriateness of this is likely to be dependent on the temperament of the dog as some dogs can become frustrated and then the enrichment device itself is counterproductive. So it is important to judge this on a case-by-case basis as there is a fine line between working for something to receive a reward and becoming frustrated with a device that will not deliver regardless of what you do. There are also activities such as scatter feeding, offering treats contained within frozen foods and using animal chews and training-based play which do not require specific devices. Some dog owners use existing toys but make these more novel with different pastes and spreads which can actually make a dog more enthusiastic about their old toys. For the more lethargic and/or older dogs treats can be hidden in the garden or around the house in order to pique their interest in exploring (the aim is for them to find these unexpectedly). Any structured training activity that an owner could do is also exercising a dog's brain and therefore is a form of enrichment. It may also be feasible to do training activities and reward-based play when an owner is out on walks with their dog, for example, scatter feeding outside or inside with dry food.

## REINFORCEMENT WITH REWARDS

Using reinforcement of behaviour with different rewards enables a change in the dog-owner relationship so that a dog learns that the owner is in control of situations (in a non-dominant way) without the need for the owners to use any physical force or demonstrate any aggressive behaviours. This process enables the dog to learn environmental predictability and they then don't need to work so hard for rewards and as a result they become more settled and more relaxed. By the owner managing the dog's resources such as food, toys and the owner's attention, they can ask the dog to perform a command such as sit before they give any of the dog's resources as a reward. In this way the owner is reinforcing their dog's expectations of their behaviour. Owner attention is often the resource that most owners do not use as they overlook the value to their dog, but it is often the resource that is the greatest value to the dog (even if it is something as simple as eye contact). Owners are often advised to reward the behaviours you want to see more of in your dog and ignore the behaviours you don't want. By following this rule, the desirable behaviours the dog shows will increase (positive reinforcement) whilst the undesirable should decrease (negative punishment). However, when an owner starts to make changes in the way they act towards their dog, their dog can become confused and this can manifest in a number of previously unseen behaviours; therefore implementing this type of change should only be done with the assistance of a qualified Animal Behaviour Consultant.

## TRAINING ACTIVITIES

It is not unusual for Animal Behaviour Consultants to be called by clients who would like their puppy trained. However, an untrained puppy does not require a behaviour modification programme but could benefit from basic training. Therefore dog trainers and dog training clubs that offer reward-based training methods are advised. It is important that owners and dogs feel comfortable and relaxed while training; otherwise it could be a process that becomes stressful and counterproductive.

## MUZZLE TRAINING

Effective muzzle usage, and therefore muzzle training, is an essential health and safety aspect of dog ownership. All dogs should be muzzled when around children and vulnerable adults and if trained appropriately it is not a welfare issue. The basket-style muzzle is recommended (it is a good idea to keep a spare one in the event of damage). When fitted properly the dog should be able to drink with it on, owners/trainers can post treats through it, and the dog should still be able to bark and pant and be comfortable exhibiting all normal behaviours. The muzzle will not only prevent a dog from being successful in any exhibition of aggressive behaviour, but it will also not be able to cause injury. As a result, the dog will be perceived as less dangerous and not cause a defensive response from people (which can paradoxically often cause some dogs to seek more interaction).

The fitting instructions should be carefully adhered to as if it is uncomfortable/ill fitted the dog will not want to wear it. The owner should make sure it is not put on abruptly or with any force or confrontation. It is better to leave it around (not for the dog to play with but for them to become familiar with it, habituation). If the dog voluntarily walks over to it and shows interest then the dog can be rewarded. The owner can gradually build up to putting it near the face for a second and then touching the nose for a second and then on for a second whilst constantly rewarding them. The owner should always take it away when things are going well and they want to interact with the dog more, rather than when the dog has had enough. The owner should slowly build up the time it is left on and reward their dog when they are relaxed with it on. If the dog makes any attempt to take it off then the owner should take a step back and repeat the process. An owner should reward their dog when wearing the muzzle and not when it is taken off. It should be noted that in the event of an owner's dog meeting another dog with an aggression disorder, then their dog would not be able to defend itself. Adequate supervision and recall training is required for dogs exercised off the lead. If a dog has shown any aggressive behaviour then it should never be left unsupervised especially when in the vicinity of children and/or vulnerable adults, even if it is wearing a muzzle. **Regardless of behaviour, all dogs should be separated and/ or muzzled and always supervised by an adult when in the presence of children and vulnerable adults.**

## SPECIFIC TREATMENT CONSIDERATIONS FOR THE CASE STUDIES COVERED IN CHAPTER 5

Treatment in the form of a behaviour modification programme is only given after a lengthy consultation with the dog owner(s) as well as anyone else in the household and/or anyone with involvement with the dogs. In most cases the dogs are seen in their usual environment as well as on a lead walk and whilst off lead. Primary treatments address the main and usually most obvious issue but tend not to be as effective without simultaneous or subsequent delivery of the secondary treatments which are implemented in case studies 1–4. **As the case studies were fictitious these particular treatments are considered but not applied.**

### CASE STUDY 1

Primary Treatment: Desensitise to the presence of Jack by starting at the point where Jack is least threatening to Sally. By doing so Victoria can offer a reward to Sally for displaying all normal behaviours and without showing any anxiety. When Sally is completely relaxed with Jack at a given distance then this distance can start to be reduced as long as Sally is unresponsive to his presence (desensitised). Victoria can continue to reward Sally. Jack needs to be careful that not only his physical distance but also his posture is non-threatening and non-communicative to Sally so that as far as she is concerned it makes no difference if Jack is present or not. Once Sally is at the point where Jack is perceived as non-threatening then she can be rewarded and encouraged to interact with him, i.e. counter-conditioning.

Secondary Treatments: enrichment techniques to make Sally place less emphasis on the people in the household. This can include the use of any of the devices already outlined in the Enrichment Techniques section. Also, there should be reinforcement with rewards to give more predictability to Sally as to how Jack and Victoria would interact with her to implement a form of balance between her perceptions of both owners.

## CASE STUDY 2

Primary Treatment: Ace's noise phobia to fireworks is motivated by fear, therefore he should benefit from being desensitised to the sounds that makes him nervous. So, the owner could purchase an audio recording with the sound of fireworks that Ace does not like and desensitise him to these sounds (his fear is likely to be time-sensitive in that it is associated with the evening, the increased number of people and the smells that are around at the time). On the first occasion the owner should play the audio with the volume at the lowest level. Remember that dogs are reported to have a wider hearing frequency than ours so it is quite possible that if the owner cannot hear it, Ace might still detect it. Therefore it is very important for the owner to use Ace's behaviour as their guide. Whilst playing the audio at the lowest level possible the owner should go about their usual activities and make sure to occasionally treat Ace if he does not show any response to the sounds. Each time the owner does this, increase the level of the noise (slowly) and as long as Ace (and indeed the other dogs) display typical behaviour continue to play the sounds. If Ace continues to show signs of anxiety, the owner would then need to reduce the volume and go back a step. The owner should continue to do this until Ace shows no signs of anxiety when the audio is being played loudly. In the event of unforeseen fireworks/thunderstorms the owner should ignore any attempts Ace makes to engage their attention, as it is really important that the owner does not reward any fearful behaviours, as this is likely to make Ace's anxieties worse.

Secondary Treatments: recall training, reinforcements with rewards to teach Wilf not to interact in a dominant way (e.g. not to shout or use physical force with Ace) with Ace given that he perceives this as punishment.

## CASE STUDY 3

Due to the dog's physical size and behaviour problems, as well as the substantial work involved in rehabilitating him, rehoming Deontay with a full behavioural disclosure is potentially workable. Given the breeds specifically mentioned in the Dangerous Dog Act 1991 some professionals might consider euthanasia an option for Deontay. As an immediate solution Bella might consider short-term foster care for Deontay or a private dog sitter or an animal charity.

## CASE STUDY 4

Whilst these dogs appear to be extra-large German Shepherds it is possible that they could have been a hybrid of a wolf dog, i.e.

a wolf that has bred with a German Shepherd, Siberian Husky or Alaskan Malamute. Wolf-dog hybrids can occur naturally (often when a female dog in oestrous either strays or intentionally mates with a male wolf) and genetic testing can be done to determine this. This situation is more likely to occur in America where there is a bigger population of non-domestic canines with a territory that may overlap with that of domestic dogs. Regardless of any genetic predetermination the strays of Spain are not eligible for treatment. The severity of this aggression was so extreme and confidently driven that it is possibly an established and reliable part of their behavioural repertoire and therefore the possibility of reoccurrence very likely. Hospital staff, police and veterinary staff are likely to consider euthanasia the appropriate action for both dogs.

## PREVENTION OF ATYPICAL BEHAVIOUR IN DOGS

Effective Puppy Socialisation, Training and Behaviour is a valuable effort in preventing behaviour problems. In a puppy up to 16 weeks is a critical period of socialisation where puppies remember all things that happen to them (good or bad), so ideally they should be exposed to all the things that they are likely to experience in their day-to-day setting. For example, if a puppy was born in an outdoor or rural environment they should be slowly familiarised to the sights and sounds of domestic and urban situations, for example, the sounds of the washing machine, Hoover, lorries on the road amongst others. The owner needs to ensure that they are not rewarding their puppy for any anxious behaviour shown in response to their new situations.

In order for an owner to prevent their puppy from developing any fears or phobias in later life their new puppy should mix with a variety of people in different circumstances.

Handling is a very important part of training. Allowing a puppy to get used to visits to the vets and having treatments or grooming is beneficial. These experiences will include looking in their mouth, cleaning teeth, looking in eyes, ears and grooming regularly so they get used to being handled. When an owner chooses to come in to a veterinary practice to buy routine wormers for example, they should bring in their dog to weigh it, or just bring it with them so the dog doesn't ever associate a visit to the vet with a bad experience. An owner should remember to make sure that their dog gets a reward for showing calm and relaxed behaviour when in the surgery. It is also very important that socialisation is done in moderation and that a puppy is rewarded for their non-anxious behaviour.

This is a perfect time for owners to get involved with training and develop good social skills as these will remain with their puppy into adult life. Generally it is better for an owner to focus on encouraging and rewarding calm and appropriate interactions with people and other animals, rather than rewarding their dog exclusively in formal training sessions, as this will produce dogs with a calm and confident temperament. Shouting, smacks, a tap on the nose, waving a rolled-up newspaper, throwing pebbles in a container, water squirters and training collars are all forms of punishment an owner should avoid as it can make their puppy develop anxiety disorders in later life.

Training sessions should be short (several five-minute sessions a day are much more effective than one hour once a week) and should focus on rewarding the puppy for good behaviour. Whilst training the owner should not physically place their puppy in the position that is being asked of, but use treats to encourage that posture and reward them **immediately** so that the puppy knows what it is they have done correctly. Rewards can start off as food-based with most dogs but can slowly be changed to a toy, play, a verbal "good dog" and even eye contact as this is a very powerful reward.

All dogs are different in their ability to learn new things so an owner may need to be repetitive in their training. However, less training is needed if the reward is appropriate, so an owner should have a selection of prioritised treats. This could be a treat bag containing some dry biscuits, small portions of cheese or some chunks of their favourite meat, which can be given as a reward depending on the difficulty of the training.

It is better to ignore bad behaviour but in instances where an owner cannot do this, they could try to use a distraction, then give their puppy a command it knows, reward it for responding appropriately to that command and then give their puppy an activity or a toy that it can engage with such as a stuffed toy or chew. This process will prevent it going back to the undesirable behaviour it was doing in the first place.

For health and safety reasons the most important command is the "recall". Owners will agree that taking their dog off the lead for the first time can be quite daunting so they need to ensure they are in a safe and reasonably confined area. The owner can then build up the amount of time and distance their dog is off the lead. It is advisable for an owner to put the lead on and off several times during the walk and do so for no apparent reason. The main focus of recall for the owner is that their dog is **always** rewarded for coming back no matter how long it takes as there is no incentive for the dog to come back to an angry owner or one that might punish them. This may be actually training their dog not to come back! A dog is more likely to come back if the process is built up from training in the home and garden, from one to ten minutes and by using the prioritised rewards. If necessary, the owner should try to make themselves more appealing by having prioritised treats and then you can reserve favourite treats for times when it has been particularly difficult to get their dog to come back to them. Off-lead practice should only be done in a confined area, indoors or in a fenced garden and only when the dog is coming consistently and reliably whilst on lead.

Much dog behaviour is undesirable to us but very typical to them. An owner needs to manage their puppy so it can exhibit typical behaviours but without affecting its health and safety. If a puppy likes to chew then the owner should provide a variety of desirable safe toys and chews which they are likely to prefer to their owner's furniture! Play pens or crates can be helpful for short-term use until old enough to be trusted on their own but locking them in these can lead to anxiety-related behaviour problems.

## HOUSE TRAINING

House training often becomes easier with age but an owner should get started as soon as possible. The owner should provide an outside area that they want their puppy to use and take them there several times per day, particularly after mealtimes. The owner should wait around until their puppy is urinating and give them verbal praise. Should an owner wish to introduce a command word when they are going to the toilet then they should do this whilst the puppy is in the act. Over time this will become associated and the dog should learn to urinate on command.

If an owner has a puppy from a rural area and it is used to urinating on sawdust, then provide some sawdust in the desired outside area. Toilet training involves spending a lot of time outside and therefore it is much easier to get a new puppy in the summer and work on outside toileting from day one. However, if this is not possible, an owner should use newspaper and move the newspaper nearer to the outside door and encourage them to go out.

By getting their puppy accustomed to being alone, an owner is preventing the development of over-attachments and therefore their puppy should not feel stressed or unsettled when they are not present. By removing the predictability of the actions that tell their puppy that the owner is leaving, they will prevent the puppy from becoming anxious before they leave and minimise any potential separation anxiety. As it is possible that a new puppy has never before been left alone, the owner should try and build up the amount of time that they are initially left for. An owner could start with a few minutes and build up to an hour and then more than one hour. An owner can also start leaving their puppy alone in a room in their home, again building up this time from a few minutes to more. How long an owner leaves their puppy or dog alone will vary depending on the breed type, the dog's temperament and the owner's personal domestic set-up.

The main thing for an owner to avoid is returning to their puppy when they are making any vocalisations or calls that are purely for attention. As long as an owner is sure that their puppy is safe and has food and/or water and has recently toileted, then they should avoid constantly responding to calls for company, as this is likely to become a learnt behaviour and is not so appealing from an adult dog when the owner is getting in the car to go to work. It is good for a puppy to learn that good things also happen when the owner is not around so before an owner leaves they should consider putting a safe style of chew or some tasty treats in a toy or in the dog's bed as this will give the dog something to do during their departure and make their absence a positive event. The first thing an owner should do is to be conscious of their routine immediately before they leave the house and try to do these things randomly during the day and night so that their puppy does not learn any triggers that warn of the owner's departure. This will have the effect of breaking any association between the owner's preparations to leave and the feelings of anxiety. For example, an owner might pick up their coat and/or keys and/or bag at various times throughout the day, then sit down and have a coffee or watch TV. During all of this, the owner should be ignoring any attention seeking behaviour that may be elicited by their puppy. In the same way that the owner is mixing up the cues that signal to their puppy that they are leaving, they can use the cues that the owner is staying home and then leave, e.g. go out in your nightgown and slippers. Owners should not offer any "bye bye" or other verbal gestures that tell their puppy they are leaving. So, when the owner does leave, it is better to be organised in advance so that you can walk out without leaving any obvious preparatory signs. On returning home it is best to avoid any big reunions and try to ignore the dog/puppy until you are in and settled, and when it has calmed down and is no longer asking for attention, ask it to sit and then say "hello".

It is important for an owner to ignore anything that their puppy may have done that they are not happy with when they come home. Dogs are extremely social and intelligent animals and can read an owner's facial signs much better than we think. Many owners report that their "dog knows" that they did something wrong when they come home but sadly, the dogs are more usually responding to their owners' behaviour in the presence of something that their owners don't like, particularly if it has resulted in a punishment for the dog in the past. It is best for an owner to ignore anything that they did not see their puppy do and prevent them from doing so again in the future.

# 7

---

# WHAT TO DO IF I NEED MORE HELP

**I am a dog owner who needs help in addressing my dog's behaviour; where do I go for help?** Firstly do not attempt to apply any of the steps involved in dog behaviour modification outlined in this book without first consulting an approved Dog Behaviour Consultant. Secondly, contact your veterinary surgeon to make sure there is no physical cause to your dog's change in behaviour. Thirdly, only ever engage in any form of dog behaviour modification in working with an approved Behaviour Consultant.

## DO:

✓ Contact your veterinary surgeon and make sure your dog has a clean bill of health
✓ Make sure your dog is insured
✓ For aggression-related behaviour, make sure your dog is muzzle trained
✓ Ask your insurance company who they recommend you go to
✓ Contact the Association for Pet Behaviour Counsellors (APBC)
✓ Contact your local reward-based dog trainer

## DO NOT:

✗ Assume your dog has a behaviour problem. Get your veterinary surgeon to check your dog for a clean bill of health.

✗ Use this book as a complete guide to resolve your dog's behaviour on your own

**I am studying animal behaviour and I want to become a Dog Behaviour Consultant; where do I go for advice and guidance?** The Association for Pet Behaviour Counsellors (APBC) offers advice on becoming a pet behaviour counsellor in the UK.

## DO:

✓ Contact your local APBC Animal Behaviour Consultant, veterinary surgery and dog trainer and get as much experience as you can watching dogs interact with their owners

✓ Read research journals such as Anthrozoos, Animal Behaviour and Applied Animal Behaviour Science

✓ Make sure you are adequately insured to work with owners and their dogs (even as a student)

✓ Make sure you consider all the health and safety aspects of working with aggressive dogs by doing a risk assessment (including wearing protective clothing and keeping your vaccines up to date)

✓ Make sure the animal behaviour course that you undertake is one which comprehensively covers all aspects of the knowledge and skills you need for your career

## DO NOT:

✗ Assume this book will equip you with enough knowledge or a skillset adequate to practice as a Dog Behaviour Consultant

# FURTHER READING

## CHILDHOOD ANIMAL CRUELTY AND ADULTHOOD VIOLENCE

Flynn, C.P. (2011) Examining the links between animal abuse and human violence. *Crime Law Social Change*, 55:453–468.

## REVIEW OF DOG OWNERSHIP AND DOG-WALKING RESEARCH

Oka, K., Shibata, A. & Ishii, K. (2014) Association of dog ownership and dog walking with human physical activity. *Journal of Physical Fitness and Sports Medicine*, 3(3):291–295.

## REVIEW OF DOG OWNERSHIP AND PHYSICAL ACTIVITY

Christian, H.E., Westgarth, C., Bauman, A., Richards, E., Rhodes, R.E., Evenson, K.R., Mayer, J.A. & Thorpe Jr, R.J. (2013) Dog ownership and physical activity: A review of the evidence. *School of Nursing Faculty Publications*, Paper 9.

## STRESS AND BEHAVIOUR

Carlson, N.R. (1998) *Physiology of Behaviour.* Allyn and Bacon.

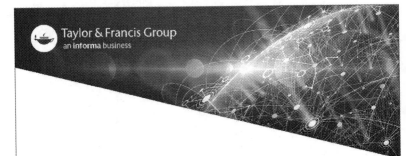

Printed in the United States
by Baker & Taylor Publisher Services